SPECIAL DELIVERY: CANADA'S POSTAL HERITAGE

Special Delivery

CANADA'S POSTAL HERITAGE

Chantal Amyot
Bianca Gendreau
John Willis

Edited by Francine Brousseau
Principal photography by Claire Dufour

GOOSE LANE EDITIONS

CANADIAN MUSEUM OF CIVILIZATION – CANADIAN POSTAL MUSEUM

Printed in Canada.
10 9 8 7 6 5 4 3 2 1

Canadian Cataloguing in Publication Data

Amyot, Chantal
Special delivery: Canada's postal heritage

Issued also in French under title: Livraison spéciale: L'héritage postal canadien.
Co-published by the Canadian Museum of Civilization and
the Canadian Postal Museum.
Includes bibliographical references and index.
ISBN 0-86492-310-4

1. Postal service — Canada — History.
2. Postal service — Canada — Equipment and supplies — History.
I. Gendreau, Bianca, 1960- II. Willis, John
III. Canadian Museum of Civilization. IV. Canadian Postal Museum. V. Title.

HE6655.A49 2000   383'.4971   C00-900869-1

Published with the financial support of the Canada Council for the Arts,
the Government of Canada through the Book Publishing Industry
Development Program, and the New Brunswick Culture and Sports Secretariat.

The Canadian Museum of Civilization and the Canadian Postal Museum
gratefully acknowledge the funding provided by Canada Post Corporation.

Goose Lane Editions
469 King Street
Fredericton, New Brunswick
CANADA E3B 1E5

Canadian Museum of Civilization
Canadian Postal Museum
100 Laurier Street
PO Box 3100, Station B
Hull, Quebec
CANADA J8X 4H2

CONTENTS

PREFACE

CANADA POST CORPORATION is proud to have contributed to the production of *Special Delivery: Canada's Postal Heritage*. This exceptional book presents a remarkable account of a service that has been bringing all Canadians closer together for at least three centuries. Canada's postal service carries our messages from coast to coast to coast and overseas as well. Letters truly know no bounds.

Writing instruments have changed extensively over the centuries, from antique quill pens to the latest personal computer. This book tells the story of these changes and the continuing role of Canada Post and the Department of the Post Office that preceded it in forwarding messages produced by these instruments for expressing human thought.

Mail delivery extends through all periods of Canadian history and provided a vital link for our pioneers, wherever they settled across this vast country. Today, Canada Post continues to take this indispensable part in strengthening the country's social and economic fabric.

The post indeed touches every Canadian. Francine Brousseau and her team have wonderfully ensured that *Special Delivery* reflects the essential service that my Canada Post colleagues offered and continue to offer, day after day, everywhere in this country.

Today, when the Internet provides a boundless catalogue of merchandise, Canadians continue to rely on their postal service to deliver the goods, just as they did a hundred years ago. From dogsleds to planes, every mode of transportation is used to move the mail. Today, EPOST™ adds cables and antennas to the more traditional methods.

I am pleased to find that *Special Delivery* reminds us of how important the mail is in the life of every Canadian. As I turn the pages of *Special Delivery*, I am proud of all the women and men who made the seventeenth- and eighteenth-century postal service, the Department of the Post Office and Canada Post Corporation an institution that has earned the trust of every Canadian each day.

The Honourable ANDRÉ OUELLET, P.C., Q.C.
President and Chief Executive Officer
Canada Post Corporation

FOREWORD

FOR SOME TIME NOW, we have shared a dream: to present the collection of the Canadian Postal Museum in a beautiful volume, a sumptuous book. We hope that you will share in our passion for the fascinating history of the post in Canada. Linked to writing and communication, mail lies at the heart of our lives and the history of our country. Inscribed in the global village, mail is universal and has no borders. Symbolized by the letter carrier, the letter or the stamp, it is part of our daily life.

The postal system has always taken part in the great historical moments of our vast country: in the fur trade, in the construction of the railway, on the battlefield, evolving with the rhythm of explorers' discoveries and the settlement of our land. The post office has been situated, literally and figuratively, right in the centre of our villages and cities; the postal service has given rise to public debates and contributed to the economy. At the dawn of the new millennium, the postal system responds to the needs of Canadians with a broad network of modern services.

The collection of the Canadian Postal Museum consists of approximately forty thousand objects and tens of thousands of philatelic items. Temporarily released from their treasure boxes, hundreds of objects and documents come alive here for the camera's eye like witnesses revealing the postal heritage of Canada. From clay tablets to the touching letter of a soldier, from the ornate decor of post offices to stamp boxes created from precious materials, through horse-and-buggy days and the golden age of catalogue shopping, we get a new perspective on Canadian history.

Postal scenes from today and yesterday lead us towards new discoveries. First, we learn about postal workers: the people who make the mail move have been and still are numbered in the thousands, and all have their stories. Another discovery is Canadian geography: the land as seen from horseback, from a stagecoach, a mail car or a plane, the country explored by whatever means used to carry the mail. We travel in all seasons, over the oceans, along the Trans-Canada Highway, on little country roads and forest trails, all the routes travelled by our messengers. We enter the territory where art and mail converge: postal bags decorated with phosphorescent designs, mail art exchanged among artists around the world, and stamps, true works of art in miniature.

Created in 1971, the Canadian Postal Museum has been part of the Canadian Museum of Civilization since 1988. Its mission is to preserve and interpret the postal heritage of Canada. *Special Delivery: Canada's Postal Heritage* invites you to discover the intriguing history of mail in Canada.

The production of a book like *Special Delivery* is the work of many hands. We are grateful to two people in particular at Canada Post: André Ouellet, who was enthusiastic from the beginning, and Alain Guilbert, our partner in design and conceptualization, who contributed tremendously to the project. We would also like to thank Canada Post for its financial assistance, without which this book would not have been possible.

We are especially grateful to two members of the Canadian Museum of Civilization Publishing Group. Jean-François Blanchette, Publisher, helped us to express our ideas more eloquently and thus create an even more fascinating book, as well as to find the best publishers for our work; and Lisa Leblanc, Co-Publication Coordinator, handled the heavy administrative load admirably and so carried this project to term. Thank you, also, to the two publishers who have collaborated to produce a lovely book that will be available throughout Canada, Goose Lane Editions and Les Éditions du Boréal. At Goose Lane, we are grateful to Susanne Alexander, Publisher, for working with Jean-François Blanchette to turn a concept into the English and French editions of a published book; to Laurel Boone, Editorial Director, for her valuable and judicious editorial work; and to Julie Scriver, Art Director, whose impeccable design skills have made it possible to present our ideas and images in their visual splendour. At Boréal, thanks go to Jacques Godbout, President, and Pascal Assathiany, General Manager, whose enthusiasm for the subject matter was obvious and who encouraged us throughout the course of the project; and to Jean Bernier, Editorial Director, for editing the French edition and for his invaluable contribution throughout the editorial process.

The items in our collection and the theme of postal history have been interpreted for you by three authors and by many powerful and eloquent images. Special thanks go to Claire Dufour, who presents the objects with great sensitivity, and for the contemporary postal scenes for which she is responsible. Thank you, also, to Steven Darby at the Canadian Museum of Civilization, and to Larry Goldstein and John Sherlock for their contemporary postal scenes.

We are especially grateful to Gaëtanne Blais and Pascal LeBlond of Services Hermès, for their help with the research and in coordinating the project. Thank you to Wendy McPeake for organizational and editorial assistance and to Jo-Anne Elder for the translation.

We would also like to acknowledge the helpful collaboration of the following people: from Canada Post, Allison Rogers, Alain Leduc and Georges de Passillé; from the Canadian Museum of Civilization, Harry Foster, Stéphane Laurin, Julie Leclair, John Staunton, the conservation team, the Canadian Ethnology Service, and the History Division; from the Canadian War Museum, Carole Reid; Jean Bélisle; Claude A. Simard; and Bernard Tousignant.

FRANCINE BROUSSEAU, Editor
Director, Canadian Postal Museum
Director of Exhibitions, Canadian Museum
 of Civilization

THE POST:
CARRIER *of the* WORD

John Willis

Mail: everyone receives it, everyone sends it, everyone waits for it. Whether it's news of a loved one at war, notification of a scholarship, a publisher's acceptance, a letter from Santa, a cheque from home, a hobby magazine, a holy relic, or an ordinary, everyday household bill, the anticipation of mail is as universal and inescapable as birth and death.

The post office is the place where we drop off our precious missives, our lovingly wrapped parcels for kids at camp, our gifts for distant family. The postal workers stand behind the wickets ready to serve. Here we buy stamps — miniatures in art, history, biology — their gummy undersides waiting to be licked and pressed onto envelopes. Conversations break out across the counter between the wicket clerk and the customer. A clerk weighs our packages, stamps them and tosses them into the bins, ready to begin the ancient journey across time and space from the unseen backrooms of the post office and processing plant to the holds of buses, trains and airplanes, to the insides of the letter carriers' bags and, finally, into the hands of the addressees.

We do not hesitate to entrust our carefully scribed notes, letters and cards, sometimes even our money, to the post office. We expect our parcels to reach their destinations. We have confidence in the ability of the post office to deliver the goods.

The Ancient Art of Communication

Communication is a total experience. Every human being uses signals to convey information or feelings. We communicate with smiles, shifting eyes, or grimaces. A shivering body says, "It's cold," or "I'm afraid."

Oral exchanges elevate the level of communication beyond the expressions of body language. Storytelling passes down moral guidance and culture and sustains the collective memory of non-literate peoples. The Six Nations Iroquois Confederacy regularly

Below: Wampum belt, Huron-Wendat Nation, from around Wendake (Loretteville, Quebec), probably early nineteenth century. Traditionally, such belts helped record a particular transaction and were exchanged at a treaty ceremony or important conference. Between events, the wampum keeper periodically brought out the belts to rehearse their messages and thus preserve the stories they told.
CMC Canadian Ethnology Service III-H-485 (CD)

Right: Ottawa post office. (SD)

Below: Reaching for the long-awaited mail in the Eastern Townships, Quebec. (Francine Brousseau)

Above: Stacks of newspapers wait to be sorted at the post office in Chicoutimi, Quebec. Archives nationales du Québec, Centre du Saguenay — Lac-Saint-Jean, Collection de la Société historique du Saguenay (P2), 10195-B

used memory aids or mnemonic devices such as the wampum belt to hold onto and honour tradition.

Talk reigns on the floor of the stock exchange, in the bazaar and at the office water cooler. "Talk, or gossip," novelist Robertson Davies wrote, "is the cud of life," which we "chew and re-chew with unfailing relish." According to Arlette Farge, historian of eighteenth-century Paris, talk was so important it was looked upon as sacred. "Mobile, swift, disfigured and disfiguring, it was talk that was the maker and breaker of friendships, creator of upheaval as well as solidarity; and talk, in spite of everything, was taken at its word."

If talk is the warp of communication, then the written word is the weft. Like a tapestry, a letter holds our intimate and private thoughts. Written on handmade paper or the back of an envelope, with a gold pen or the stub of a pencil, sealed with wax or glue, the letter may be confidential, yet rarely is the content of a letter shared only by the two communicators. Entire families might listen in as a letter is read out loud. Empires may fall, businesses may flourish, careers may be launched, all by virtue of a letter.

A letter can convey a very public message. The editorial pages of Canada's newspapers have always been the stage for enthusiastic — and frequently heated — expressions of social and political opinion. In the mid-twentieth century, women's-page columnists responded to anonymous letters asking for advice on everything from moral and ethical issues to troubles of the heart ("Is it a crime to be married to a man you're not in love with?") to practical information like how to get an ink stain out of your best silk blouse.

Today's postal system is an elaborate and complex system of local post offices, processing plants and an international mail-delivery network. Whatever the form or intention of a letter, when it is dropped into a mailbox the sender has faith that it will reach its destination anywhere in the world. This unquestioned confidence is the legacy of an international postal system that is the centuries-old precursor to McLuhan's global village.

The postal horn, one of the oldest symbols associated with the post, is often depicted on postal heraldic insignia. In 1832, the couriers who travelled up the Ottawa River from Montreal blew horns to announce the arrival of the mail. CPM 1974.1310.1 (CD)

North America, Europe, South America, Australia, and Asia are represented as five messengers in the emblem of the Universal Postal Union. This elegant sculpture is a replica of the large bronze and granite statue created in Bern, Switzerland, by Charles-René de Paul de Saint-Marceaux to commemorate the twenty-fifth anniversary of the UPU. CPM 1974.1317.1 (CD)

The Universal Postal Union

In 1875, twenty-two countries founded the Universal Postal Union (UPU) in Bern, Switzerland, to regulate the international mail stream; Canada joined in 1878. The UPU was one of the modern world's first international organizations. Standard rates and procedures were gradually established to handle the growing volume of letters, parcels and money orders flowing between independent countries. Letters posted from one country to another bore blue postage stamps, their denominations inscribed in Arabic numerals, a factor in moving the world toward a common numerical language.

In 1907, the UPU reduced the cost of sending letters internationally to twenty-five centimes for the first twenty-five grams or five cents for the first ounce. The Postmaster General of Canada confidently asserted, "In writing a letter abroad of moderate length, it will no longer be necessary to use paper so thin as to make the writing almost illegible, and if one wants to send a heavier letter, the diminution in the charge will be very considerable." This measure made it easier for the growing immigrant population of Canada to keep in touch with the old country. All of a sudden, the world became a smaller place.

Today the UPU numbers 189 members and has become the manager of international postal business. As a symbol of world-wide postal co-operation, the UPU reminds us of the many and varied postal links between Canada and the rest of the world.

Below left: Behind the scenes at the Vancouver mail processing plant. (LG)

Bottom: In the 1940s, the mail brought the news to the nation. CPM (CD)

Below: Newsboy selling papers on street, circa 1905. Notman Photographic Archives, McCord Museum of Canadian History, Montreal, MP-0000.586.112

Right: Inside the mail processing plant, Halifax, Nova Scotia, a friendly letter carrier sorts the mail. (JS)

Centre: Signs of the ubiquitous presence of the post office. CPM (CD)

Below right: Lining up to mail parcels, 1928. NAC/PA-061991 (Eugene M. Finn)

Above: Filling out a money order at the Ottawa post office. (SD)

Legacy of the Past

In ancient civilizations, the written word was a conqueror of space and time. Imbued with political power and influence, no ruler could afford to ignore it or neglect it. "The pen and the sword worked together," wrote Harold Innis. "The written word, signed, sealed and swiftly transmitted, was essential to military power and the extension of government."

Throughout the Nile Valley, royal messengers of ancient Egypt carried messages inscribed on papyrus. Information flowed smoothly throughout the Persian Empire as horsemen moved dispatches for their ruler, Cyrus the Great, back and forth between the capital city of Babylon and regularly spaced stops, or *hippones*. Similarly, the Roman *cursus publicus* operated along a network of carefully planned relay stations, or *mutationes*, located every twelve kilometres. In Japan, along the Tokaido between Tokyo and Kyoto, fifty-three stations accommodated travellers and messengers.

As late as the sixteenth century, information moved slowly along fixed routes. Stopping places at one-day intervals along the road between Istanbul and the Balkans were known as *caravanserai*. Here people slept on platforms along the sides of buildings while the horses were awarded the choice places in the middle. The speed with which news travelled from anywhere in Europe to Venice, Fernand Braudel reminds us, increased very little from 1500 to 1765, the maximum being one hundred kilometres per day. Only the richest cities could afford to build and maintain roads that made faster travel possible.

Messengers seldom ventured outside established corridors because these routes provided the necessities of travel: stables, food and lodging. At sea, too, ships stopped at appointed ports of call to take on food and water and to exchange mail, rarely straying from their established routes.

Heraldic symbol of the Post Office of Canada. CPM 1974.2153.1 (CD)

Reproduction of a postal stone dating from 1635, now in the South African Cultural History Museum. As ships rounded the Cape of Good Hope to and from the Indian colonies, the crews would come ashore and leave letters beneath such stones in the hope that a ship going the other way would pick them up. On occasion, they left messages on the stones themselves. CPM LH96.15.1 (CD)

THE mechanical affixing of postage stamps and sealing envelopes has for years been standard practice wherever efficient office methods prevail. The operation of the Mailometer is exceedingly simple. It can be used for sealing and stamping together or in separate operations, as desired.

During the early modern period, specialized postal systems emerged. Some, like those in England and France, were managed by the state. A private initiative sponsored by the Hapsburgs laid the foundations for the postal monopoly of Thurn and Taxis in south and central Europe. Beginning in the fifteenth century, this postal monopoly handled all the mail throughout the Hapsburg Empire from Italy to the Netherlands and from Sicily to Spain. As in the ancient empires of Persia and Rome, a postal network for the exchange of information along fixed, safe itineraries was imperative to the maintenance of power.

Getting and maintaining power was a constant impetus for postal development throughout the history of ancient and modern civilizations. But, after the fall of the Roman Empire in the mid-fifth century, power in Europe was never again concentrated in a single authority. Other sources of postal initiative came to the fore. During the medieval era, monasteries, universities and town corporations developed their own postal messenger systems. Later, merchants of the leading Italian trading cities — principally Venice and Genoa — were anxious to ensure the safe transmission of money, information and goods. They devised a decentralized system of commercial control and information distribution involving a network of agents based in various parts of the expanding world economy. Collectively, the agents constituted a human chain that was the backbone of

Letter carrier delivering Super Mike's mail, Halifax, Nova Scotia.
(JS)

the informal postal system. It was this same informal postal chain that Champlain and his successors brought to North America and that formed the beginnings of postal communication in New France.

This system in turn laid the foundation for Canada's modern postal institution, which can be traced back to the British colonial period. Following Confederation, the system was centralized under the authority of a single branch of the Dominion government of Canada, the Post Office Department, which implemented a national postal service. Stagecoaches, trucks, railway mail cars, and eventually airplanes moved mail across the country and around the world. So pervasive is its reach and so grand is its appearance that the mail system has gradually been internalized into popular culture.

The postal system is more than a means of letter distribution. As an institution it is constantly being made and remade in the image of its patrons and its workers, from the clerks who sort the mail to the letter carriers who faithfully deliver the mail from house to house, to the postmasters who serve rural communities. The post is a recurrent cycle of communication in which each message gives birth to another. The ebb and flow of messages and replies helps us keep in touch with all the things that matter in our world.

PUTTING PEN TO PAPER

Bianca Gendreau

Writing was born in Mesopotamia, in western Asia, about five thousand years ago. Sumerians invented the first signs representing concrete realities — objects used in daily life, animals, parts of the body, and so on — and scribes used these pictograms to keep accounts and record events. Throughout the centuries, the scribes modified this writing system until complex characters and groups of characters evolved that could convey abstract ideas as well as signifying objects.

The act of writing engages both the senses and the intellect and requires nothing more than a small number of simple tools. In Mesopotamia, scribes impressed their accounts or inventories on clay tablets with a *calamus*, a sharpened reed, and so cuneiform writing (the characters resemble nails, *cuneus* in Latin) developed. The impressed tablets were sometimes covered by a second layer of clay on which the scribes would impress the names of the recipients or transcribe the message again. It goes without saying that these missives were rather fragile.

Although clay tablets were used in Mesopotamia for more than two thousand years, other writing surfaces developed in ancient times, each civilization creating its own from whatever material was readily available. In Egypt and China, people wrote on stone, papyrus or silk. The invention of a means of producing papyrus from the fibres of the papyrus reed, which grew on the banks of the Nile, was a major advance in the technology of written communication. From Egypt, where it was used more than three thousand years before the birth of Christ, this ancestor of paper spread throughout the Mediterranean basin area.

But wooden tablets covered in wax, less costly than papyrus, were also used throughout the Roman Empire; these tablets were the principal writing surface in the empire until the appearance of parchment. First, a tablet was carved out, leaving a lip around the

Below: Fragment of a letter written on papyrus in the fourth century AD. CPM 1974.2132.1 (CD)

Facing page: Writing case and writing supplies from the end of the nineteenth century. CPM 1999.76.1.0 (CD)

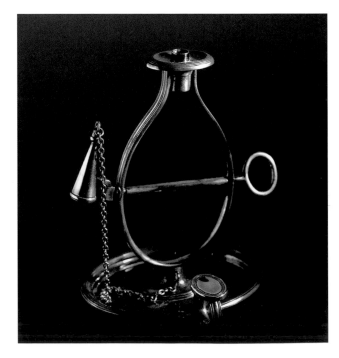

edge so that wax could be poured into it; a second tablet served as a lid or cover. A small tool called a stylet, made of bone, metal or ivory, was used to write on the wax. One end of the stylet was pointed, and the other was shaped like a spatula, enabling the writer to erase characters by rubbing the wax down. The recipient could erase the message and write a reply on the same tablet.

Parchment, invented in Pergamon, a city in Asia Minor, started gaining in popularity in the second century BC. By the beginning of the Middle Ages, it had replaced Egyptian papyrus, which was rare and expensive, and the cumbersome wax tablets. Made of animal skin, parchment was thin, flexible, easy to handle, and light to carry, and it became the writing surface of choice for monastic copyists of scriptures, missals and other prayer books, as well as for official documents and letters. As well as their pens, writers on parchment also used other supplies and tools, including ink and inkwells and chisels or sharp knives to score the parchment and scratch out errors. Before beginning their work, they prepared the page of parchment, that is, they calculated the writing surface and the margins necessary if the writing was to be bound into a book, and they marked out one, two or even three columns.

Although clay tablets quickly fell out of use, silk, papyrus, wax tablets and parchment were used concurrently until the end of the Middle Ages. Paper was invented by the Chinese about two thousand years ago, but it did not conquer the world for a long time.

Turning the Pages

Paper arrived in the western world during the eleventh and twelfth centuries, spreading throughout Europe with the Arab conquests. The advent of the printing press in the fifteenth century marked the decline of parchment, and paper then became the material used nearly exclusively as a surface for all forms of writing.

Until factory-produced envelopes arrived on the market around 1850, letter writers used an elegant means of sealing their epistles. They simply folded the sheet of paper and applied hot wax on the fold; once it hardened, the wax was a guarantee of privacy.

Personal seals allowed their possessors to impress their coat of arms or initials in the warm wax. The seal was generally engraved in a metal such as silver or in a gemstone such as agate, emerald or ruby. These were, obviously, luxury objects. While most were rather heavy and intended to be desktop decorations, some were finely chiselled and could be carried in a pocket or worn on a chain like a jewel.

In the middle of the nineteenth century, letter paper was generally small — thirteen by eighteen centimetres was a standard size — and was sold in packages of twenty-four or twenty-five sheets. Despite the principles taught in writing

Below left: Title page and frontispiece from The Fashionable Letter Writer, or, The Art of Polite Correspondence, *by B.A. Turner (London: Dean & Munday and A.K. Newman [188?]). Very popular in the nineteenth century, such manuals for the uninspired gave examples of letters and replies for every imaginable circumstance and also provided advice on etiquette and decorum.* Musée de la civilisation, bibliothèque du Séminaire de Québec, fonds ancien (Jacques Lessard)

Above: Knife from the middle of the nineteenth century. CPM 1986.85.4 (CD)

manuals, letter writers often wrote first across the page and then lengthwise on the same page to save paper. Paper merchants and printers responded to the needs of their growing clientele with fine writing papers, waffled or monogrammed stationery, announcements and black-bordered mourning stationery. Coloured paper had the reputation of being less distinguished than white, but even so, it was widely used for personal correspondence and could be ordered from mail-order catalogues.

When valentine cards first became popular near the end of the nineteenth century, they were decorated with floral borders. Their country scenes, flying birds or mixed bouquets give them an old-fashioned charm to modern eyes.

The Victorians adored rituals, and their social code directed the course of daily life. Love was necessarily romantic. Courtship, carried out with great care, included the art of letter-writing. Letters of introduction, guest cards and invitations were all part of this art, and the suitor had to show good taste and sincerity. If a young man needed help, he could count on manuals and etiquette books; newspapers and magazines also published such instruction.

Right: A nineteenth-century embossed brass travelling inkstand containing writing supplies. CPM 1993.77.1 (CD)

Collection of inkwells. As the complex designs and the rich materials suggest, inkwells were often a status symbol or a lavish gift. CPM (CD)

Be My Valentine

Sending St. Valentine's Day cards became a vital part of the courtship ritual. Valentines were usually sent to sweethearts but were also sometimes sent to friends as a token of affection. The first valentines were hand-made, and senders would write poems in them describing their sentiments. They could purchase manuals containing romantic, light or humorous little verses that could be copied onto cards. These guides included lines written especially for soldiers, single people, husbands and wives, young people and the elderly.

The first commercial valentines appeared around 1840. Typically Victorian, these were sumptuous in their design, with intertwined hearts made of silk, paper lace, embroidered satin or even velvet, sometimes decorated with ribbons. On some, the ribbons were tied into several bows, or the bows would be laid out in the shape of a heart.

People seemed to have a weakness for cupids whose invisible arrows pierced the hearts of the valentine couple. Harps signified harmony, golden doves testified to happy marriages, and birds preparing their nests on leafy branches symbolized fertility. Some valentine cards were so elaborate and delicate that they had to be sent in boxes to protect them.

Starting in 1898, Canadians could also buy illustrated post cards. Very

Commercial valentines (top) made of paper lace, dating from the 1840s, and a heart-shaped magnifying glass.
CPM 1998.94.1 (CD)

quickly, these little rectangles of cardboard, nicknamed "the little queen of the mail" or "the poor man's telephone," became immensely popular with correspondents and collectors alike; a real passion developed for them.

Take Up Your Pens!

The form of writing that developed in China called for the use of a small brush. Brushes, brush-holders made of ivory or rock crystal, lacquerware writing cases decorated with gold leaf, and porcelain water jars from various times in the past prove that this civilization has always attributed a ritual value to the act of writing.

In the west, for many centuries, the most common writing instruments were quills, particularly those made from goose feathers. First, the barbs were carefully removed, then the sides were trimmed down into a hollow curve (this is still the characteristic shape of metal nibs on fountain pens). Then the end was cut off to form the perfect angle for writing. The flexibility of the feather made it much sought-after as a writing instrument, but this advantage was also a disadvantage, because the feather wore down quickly and had to be constantly resharpened. Long established as the royalty of writing instruments, quills gradually gave up their place of privilege to metal nibs in the nineteenth century, although the first ones were stiff, rusted easily and could not be used for very long.

To eliminate the unfortunate errors that slipped into written text, a small metal — sometimes silver — knife was used to scratch out mistakes. This would damage the paper, making the filed spots unusable. So "pounce," a fine powder of chalk, ground fish scales or bone, would be spread on the page and smoothed out over the paper with a piece of agate.

But whether one wrote with a quill or a metal nib, the writing instrument still had to be dipped again and again into the inkwell. Each new charge of ink would create dark characters, but gradually the letters would fade until a new ink supply made the next few letters dark again. Sometimes the author would get carried away with enthusiasm for his subject and forget to dip his quill often enough, so that several words would be nearly illegible and have to be deciphered in the scratches made by the dry tip. At times, the letter writer was conscious of this and apologized in his missive. Having to interrupt their writing so often must have bothered correspondents considerably, and so the rudimentary nature of the instrument was improved upon: pens with their own ink supply were invented.

There were a number of experiments with this idea. The first really successful one is attributed to an American insurance agent, Lewis Edson Waterman, who

Magnificent bronze inkwell manufactured by Tiffany in the 1920s and belonging to a lumber baron from the Ottawa Valley. CPM 1994.141.1 (CD)

Mother-of-pearl and glass penholders and fountain pens. CPM (CD)

perfected a tube that allowed ink to drip down gradually to the tip of the nib while air came up towards the reservoir. On February 12, 1884, he patented his first version of the fountain pen. At the 1889 Paris World's Fair, he launched thirty thousand of them onto the market. Little by little, other self-inking pens appeared, such as models with levers or pumps marketed by Walter A. Sheaffer in 1908 and George Parker's self-fillers. All of these were widely distributed.

With the arrival of the fountain pen, the ceremony of writing, which required skill and patience, became a routine activity. At the beginning of the twentieth century, the fountain pen was an indispensable tool, a symbol of refinement and good taste. A spirit of fantasy took hold of the manufacturers, and models made of different metals, with textured and glossy finishes, began to appear. The first fountain pens made of coloured plastic also became available.

World War I marked a turning point in the market: for one thing, the volume of mail increased substantially, and, for another, the fountain pen was a gift that was practical and portable, one of the few personal possessions that soldiers could carry with them in the trenches.

With the appearance of the ink cartridge in the middle of the 1930s, the problems with various ink-filling systems were resolved. Refills were now clean, safe and easy to carry, and the ink level was visible. A few years later the traditional writing instruments — inkwell, pen-wiper, penholders — had practically disappeared.

The fountain pen remained quite popular until the 1940s, when the ballpoint pen began to supplant it. The ballpoint nib consisted of a small metal marble that moved smoothly around the end of a narrow

A rare travelling inkstand from the end of the eighteenth century. CPM 1994.54.2 (CD)

Right: Letters — we love to write them, we love to receive them. (JS)

Below: Writing set given to a lady named Juliette Labelle in 1915, as the handwritten note accompanying the little box explains. CPM 1999.75.1.0 (CD)

Bottom: Underwood typewriter, 1923-1924. CPM 1994.163.1 (CD)

Left: Collection of erasers: accessories designed for the young. CPM (CD)

Below: Handwritten letter and Waterman Safety fountain pen, 1907. CPM 2000.14.40 (CD)

Bottom: Even today, we continue to write. Only the writing instruments have changed. (JS)

tube of ink. The first models had appeared in 1895, but a Hungarian named Lazlo Biro, living in Argentina, marketed the ballpoint pen so widely that it became known as the Biro, and this term is still used in some parts of the world.

Although the typewriter was invented in England in 1714, the first commercially practical models became available only in the 1870s. Typewriters became common in homes after World War II, and today computers are ubiquitous in business places and popular at home as well. Even so, it is still considered good manners to send handwritten thank-you notes and letters of sympathy, and handwritten personal letters are treasured today for the writer's extra effort and sincerity.

Now distributed by the thousands every day, letters remain our ambassadors, travelling to the four corners of the world. In our era of telephones and electronic mail, the thoughtful and personal touch of a letter is still appreciated. And letters last: they can be read and reread, handled again and again or tucked under a pillow if the message is from a loved one. We often describe the pleasure of getting correspondence in our mail; we know we could never become indifferent to it.

THE COLONIAL ERA:
BRINGING *the* POST
to NORTH AMERICA

John Willis

Beginning in the seventeenth century and for the next two hundred years, Canada was a colony, first of France and then of England. Communication was an adjunct to the imperial purpose. Until the early nineteenth century, this purpose was the exploitation of commodities such as fur, fish and wheat, and classes of people, including farmers, fishermen and indigenous peoples. Corridors of power, communication and trade in early Canadian history were corridors of commercial exploitation, and it was in the shadow of these power relationships that postal communications were first established.

The French and the Beginnings of the Canadian Postal System

In the seventeenth and eighteenth centuries, the French acquired considerable territory in North America. The extension of French commerce and power across the continent — south to Louisiana, northeast to Louisbourg (Acadia), and west into the Upper Country (the territory around and beyond the Great Lakes) — was a singular achievement. The communication strategy established by the French enabled them to overcome the very difficult challenge of preserving their vast empire. The strategy involved three connecting systems: transatlantic shipping, the routes and transportation infrastructure of the fur trade, and road and river travel in the St. Lawrence valley.

A quill, ink bottle and inkwell on a map: tools of the French occupation of North America. Ink bottle: CPM 1994.46.1; Inkwell: CMC History Division 988.29.91; Map: NAC/NMC-0021100 (CD)

Facing page: Late seventeenth-century Mazarin writing desk. The leather case bears Louis XV's monogram; it was probably used by messengers acting under royal authority. Musée des Augustines de l'Hôtel-Dieu de Québec. (CD)

An eighteenth-century frigate that could have brought mail from France to the colonies. National Library of Canada

Unknown, Portrait d'homme, *red chalk on paper, 14.5 x 11.1 cm.* Musée du Québec 67.202 (Patrick Altman)

In the seventeenth and eighteenth centuries, the exchange of correspondence between France and its colony across the Atlantic was dependent on the vagaries of changing seasons and wind, weather and current in the North Atlantic. Throughout most of the winter, there was virtually no means of getting mail in or out of the St. Lawrence valley. It was extremely dangerous for ships to sail the frigid waters of the Gulf of St. Lawrence in November and December, when ice began to accumulate. On November 6, 1725, the *Marie Anne* left Quebec City en route to Martinique. When the ship ran aground in the Lower St. Lawrence off the westernmost tip of Isle Verte, the captain, André Corneille, and his crew were forced to spend the winter ashore. Jean Riou, the seigneur of Trois-Pistoles, and his family helped the eleven-man crew with the necessary repairs, and they were able to set sail in September of the following year. Who knows how much mail spent the winter of 1725-1726 in Canada? In 1727, to prevent just this kind of accident, the French marine minister, Jean Frédéric Phélippeaux, comte de Maurepas, instructed colonial officials not to delay the departure of ships beyond October 20.

Cut off from France throughout the winter, colonial correspondents were anxious to receive the first mail of the season, which usually arrived in June or July. Small wonder that local riverboats frequently accosted the incoming ships offering to take in the mail, a practice that often included the opening of everyone's mail. In July 1732, Intendant Hocquart put a stop to this practice. Henceforth, ships' captains were ordered to deliver their charge of letters to an appointed place on land in order to guarantee the confidentiality of the correspondence.

In spite of transport limitations and the absence of a formal postal system, the colonists were nonetheless able to adapt, and they invented ingenious ways of ensuring mail deliveries. Travellers regularly carried mail on behalf of others. Arrangements were made with ship captains and further afield with agents in various French ports, who undertook to ensure that the mail arrived at its final destination. Thus developed the informal postal system, a human chain that enabled mail to flow back and forth across the Atlantic.

Within continental New France, a similar human network of communication was established. It linked the far-flung interior possessions of the French empire in North America to the core

The French acquired most of their geographical knowledge from the indigenous peoples, who also used their own technology to act as couriers. They carried dispatches on behalf of royal officials, and, more importantly, they brought the most up-to-date gossip to the forts, missions and towns they visited.
CMC Canadian Ethnology Service: Snowshoe III-E-83 a; Moccasins III-E-5 a-b (CD); Illustrations: Louis Armand baron de La Hontan. *Nouveaux voyages de M. Le Baron de Lahontan dans l'Amérique septentrionale* (La Haye, Chez les Frères l'Honoré, 1715, pages 34 and 72). Stewart Museum at the Fort, Île Sainte-Hélène, Montreal, Quebec.

settlements of the St. Lawrence valley through the transportation network that served the fur trade.

The fur-trade routes were developed, staffed and provisioned by the French and their native allies. During the 1720s, Father Pierre-François-Xavier de Charlevoix, explorer, teacher and high-ranking Jesuit official in Paris, travelled from Canada to Detroit, into the Mississippi drainage basin via Lake Michigan, and all the way down to New Orleans. His accounts of his travels added substantially to the geographical knowledge of those setting out the best portages and canoe routes. Although his information was sometimes inaccurate, it helped the French to carve up the vast territories into manageable itineraries. Each of the routes could be covered in a matter of days, thereby facilitating the relatively efficient movement of people and mail.

Getting the mail from the Upper Country all the way to France was no easy task. Canoes laden with furs and letters could not travel until the ice melted in April or later, and they had to arrive in Quebec before the departure of the ships for France in October; these two schedules were not easily coordinated. Due to less daunting travel arrangements, the inhabitants of the St. Lawrence valley were served by a more regular postal schedule.

Most of the mail destined for the St. Lawrence valley moved aboard sailing craft that navigated the St. Lawrence River between Montreal and Quebec City.

*A letterbox from the
1820s belonging to the* Lady
Sherbrooke. *Built in 1817, the* Lady
Sherbrooke *was John Molson's fourth
steamboat. Carrying passengers, cargo, farm
produce and mail up and down the St. Lawrence
River, the vessels of the Molson line and their competitors
could make the trip between Montreal and Quebec City in just
twenty hours. Letter writers of this era often referred to "steamboat
mail."* Private collection (CD)

The governor and intendant commissioned a *patron de chaloupe*, or chief boatman, to carry messages on their behalf in 1733. On land, as early as the 1690s, royal messengers had been commissioned to carry official mail. Their work was made considerably easier by the construction of the King's Road along the St. Lawrence River and inland during the 1730s. It became the backbone of an elaborate communication and transportation network that would eventually include post houses, stage lines and inns. Letters and gossip moved quickly along this eighteenth-century grapevine.

Because of these extensive land- and river-based systems, the people of New France came to expect their mail to be delivered, although perhaps with some delay. This expectation of regular, if informal, service was the outstanding postal legacy of the French regime, a service continued and enhanced by the British.

The British: Advent of a Formal Postal System

Postal communication underwent considerable change in the time of the British. Beginning in 1763, a formal postal service was introduced to the St. Lawrence valley. Postal routes were laid out, post offices were built, and a formal authority in the person of the Deputy Postmaster General was appointed to oversee the entire system.

Contemporary and late-nineteenth-century photos of a former stage-house on the King's Road, Deschambault, Quebec, a stop on the stage and sleigh route between Quebec City and Montreal. Winter would have been a busy time of year for the inns and post houses on the King's Road because the St. Lawrence River was impassable from late November until May.
(CD [inset]; Private collection)

Full-rigged wood and plastic model of the Marquis of Salisbury, *which carried mail between Falmouth, England, and Halifax, Nova Scotia, in the 1820s. The Falmouth packet was organized as a transatlantic postal route between Falmouth and New York in 1755, and the ships called at Halifax on their way to and from New York.* CPM 1974.1318.1 (CD)

In Nova Scotia, imperial postal authority was wielded by a succession of Deputy Postmasters General charged with the important task of sending the transatlantic winter mail from Canada to Britain. The service was introduced in 1785; mails travelled overland by sleigh or cart once a month between Quebec City and Halifax, twice monthly in summer. In the following decade, a formal arrangement reached with American officials allowed for the transmission of mail between the colonies and Great Britain via New York, thus eliminating the seasonal log jams that had previously brought the exchange of mail to a virtual standstill in winter. Because of the New York and Halifax connections, British colonists could now depend on a much more flexible and reliable postal timetable.

The establishment of a formal postal authority was not the only change during the late eighteenth and early nineteenth centuries to affect communications in the colonies. During this period, the printed word became increasingly important in the daily life and culture of the colonists. Books, newspapers and letter writing fostered the growth of various religious and political constituencies, and the postal service lubricated the circulation of news and opinions.

Monsignor Jean-Jacques Lartigue, the Bishop of Montreal, espoused very traditional views about obedience to episcopal authority in church affairs and loyalty to king and colonial authority in civil ones. Yet he fought his battles with modern tools. He was an avid reader of books and newspapers, and he corresponded by post with his ecclesiastical superior, the Bishop of Quebec City, and the parish priests under his charge, frequently on a daily basis. His successor, Ignace Bourget, made a science of gathering episcopal information through the post. Around 1841, he sent out printed forms on which the parishes of his diocese reported their activities, and then they returned them by post. By the 1850s, use of these forms became standard church procedure.

For the colonists, the post was an essential tool for conducting business. Except for face-to-face conversations, there was no better way to get information, place orders or exchange money. The import-export firm of Robertson-Masson

Below left: Example of an impressed stamp used on newspapers before they were sent abroad. Provincial Archives of New Brunswick, P110-795

Below: Notice for Charles Willmer's American News Letter, *a compendium of facts and articles drawn from the British and European press for North American readers, in the* Bytown Gazette, *February 13, 1845.* National Library of Canada, NL-22101

Below: Masthead of the Montreal newspaper, La Minerve, *September 6, 1827. Distributed by post and through a network of agents,* La Minerve *was a pillar of the Lower Canadian* patriote *movement, which opposed the British.* National Library of Canada, NL-22103

CHARLES WILLMER,
Newspaper, Forwarding, and General Agent.

CONTINUES to supply, to order, with greater promptitude and regularity than any other house, and on the most reasonable terms, (a London Daily Paper for £6 10s. Sterling per annum.) Newspapers, Prices Currents, Shipping Lists, Magazines, Books, and Stationery, Type, Printers' and Binders' Materials, and Merchandise of every description, to all parts of the United States, Canada, Nova Scotia, New Brunswick, and Newfoundland, by the Mail Steamers, sailing on the 4th and 19th of each month from Liverpool, and to all the West Indian Islands, Mexico, and Texas, by the Royal Mail Steamers, sailing every Fortnight from Southampton.

CHARLES WILLMER'S
AMERICAN NEWS LETTER

IS published for transmission by every Steam Ship sailing from England for America, and its leading feature is to give, *at a glance*, an account of every important event that has occurred in Great Britain, Europe, or Asia, in the Interval between the sailing of each Steam Ship, whether in politics or commerce—a correct and comprehensive Shipping List, in which will be found a faithful record of the arrival and departure of American vessels at and from all the British, European, and Asiatic ports, with notices of such casualties or disasters as may from time to time occur—a complete Prices Current, in which the greatest care is taken to give the *latest* reports of the markets for the various descriptions of American Produce, from the most unquestionable sources—thus combining, in *one* sheet, a *Newspaper*, a *Shipping List*, and a *Prices Current*.

Annual Subscription, payable in advance, 12s. 6d. Sterling.

All orders must be accompanied with a remittance or reference in England for payment.

NOTICE.

All communications must be post paid, & addressed

CHARLES WILLMR'S
Transatlantic Newspaper Office,
5, South John Street, LIVERPOOL.

Or they will not reach Charles Willmer's Office.
NO connexion with Messrs. Willmer & Smith.

LA MINERVE.

MONTREAL, JEUDI, LE 6 SEPTEMBRE, 1827.

ET PUBLIÉE PAR

DUVERNAY,
St. Jean Baptiste.

DITIONS.

e deux fois par semaine, le
L'abonnement est de QUATRE
tre les frais de la Poste lorsque
par cette voie, et payable A
ours de chaque Semestre.
t discontinuer leur abonnement
au moins un mois avant l'ex-
tre, et payer leurs arrérages,
sidérés comme souscripteurs
t.

reçus avec reconnaissance et
tre. Ceux qui ne seront pas
ns écrites seront insérées jus-
bités en conséquence.
réal, au bureau du Journal,
ise de Messrs. Fabre & Cie.
ens.

LA MINERVE.
Kamouraska.

VARIÉTÉS.

M. Charles Fromont s'est fait une réputation en Belgique par des épigrammes, des satires et des élégies. Les deux volumes qui viennent de paraître, forment le recueil des différentes compositions qu'il a successivement publiées; aussi l'on y trouve une agréable variété qui annonce une flexibilité heureuse de talent. On doit féliciter le poète d'avoir presque toujours pris pour sujets de ses chants les malheurs de la Grèce et les grands événemens qui ont agité l'Europe; les désastres d'Ipsara lui ont inspiré une élégie, dont nous regrettons de ne pouvoir donner ici que le commencement:

Oui, je crois à la liberté;
Je crois à ses bienfaits, je crois à ses prodiges;
De tant d'illusions j'ai vu fuir les prestiges!
Et c'est le seul qui m'est resté.
Mais tous ne sont pas faits pour elle;
Il faut un pur encens; il faut de nobles cœurs,
Ce ne sont pas des vœux, ce ne sont pas des pleurs
Qui font arriver l'immortelle;
Insensible au cri des douleurs,
C'est le glaive à la main qu'elle veut qu'on l'appelle.
Le frivole habitant des campagnes d'Enna,
Qui murmure et sourit, qui s'indigne et se cache,
Qui s'incline en rebelle et se révolte en lâche,
Crut l'aimer, et la profana.
Mais d'autres, grâce aux dieux, l'ont aimée et servie

Voyage aux Indes Occidentales p

Nous apprenons par une lettre commandant le bateau à vapeur voyage de Falmouth (Angleterre 57 jours. Pendant 35 jours, il vapeur, il s'est arrêté 3 jours à S 19 jours à l'aide des voiles. A l'ouest entre les tropiques comm il a suivi d'assez près la côte du où il a mouillé, est sous l'équ continent. La machine à vape huit mesures (de 36 boisseaux) Le charbon emporté d'Angleterre trajet, mais Mr. Johnson décla l'économiser, lui a fait perdre les propriétaires du vaisseau d'en Madère et autant à St.-Hélène. pour deux journées de charb le Capt. et qu'il avait vogué 36 j doit regarder comme constant qu faisant 8 milles par heure dans un construit et courut de manière à porter pou tible. Ce fait n'est pas sans impor distance parcourue en un jour 190 milles et par la vapeur de 16

Cover from the colonial period and nibbed pen. CPM 1983.192.18, 1999.98.20 (CD)

had partners working out of Quebec City, Montreal and Glasgow, Scotland. Accounts, bills of exchange and other financial transactions were sent back and forth across the Atlantic by mail. Agents sent out to settle accounts with local shopkeepers in various parts of Upper and Lower Canada thus kept in touch with the Montreal office. Written instructions could be mailed by travelling agents while they were in the field to the firm's attorney in Perth, Upper Canada.

Of course, the mail could not move about by itself; it had to be transported. The post came to be an important customer of the various means of transportation available to the public, and thus the postal service encouraged the growth of the transport system.

Mail contracts issued by the Deputy Postmaster General helped foster the establishment of stagecoach lines along the routes between Upper and Lower Canada and up and down the St. John River valley in New Brunswick. Mail contracts also contributed to the growth of regular sail- and then steam-powered navigation across the Bay of Fundy between Digby and Saint John. Stagecoaches and ships carried all manner of cargo, including mail, passengers and money. They favoured the flow of news as well as goods and services between towns and hinterlands and between regions.

During the 1830s and 1840s, the integration of colonial space put increased pressure on the postal system. The colonists came to realize that they required a postal system that was more appropriate to their domestic needs and more in keeping with the momentum towards self-government. The press was particularly insistent on the need for a cheap and efficient postal system, fanning the flames of postal reform and helping to insure that the post would be part of the new relationship being forged between British North America and London, the seat of Empire.

Stationary for Sale.

A FEW REAMS OF SUPERIOR
FOOLSCAP, POT AND POST PAPER,
For Sale by the Ream or half Ream.
—ALSO—
A few Dozen INK POWDERS of the best quality.
Apply at this Office.
Bytown, 10th July, 1837.

PAPIER, LIVRES, &c. &c.

DERNIEREMENT reçu de la manufacture de St. ANDRE', et à vendre par le soussigné, vis-à-vis du Séminaire de Montreal, dans la maison ci-devant occupée par James Brown, dans la même branche de commerce :

    50 Rames de grand papier à envelloppe,
    50 do   de papier à cartouche,

Qui joint à son assortiment ordinaire de papier à imprimer, à écrire et à envelloppe et de papier bleu, de différentes grandeurs et de différentes qualités, offre un assortiment très complet dans cette ligne de commerce.

Il a aussi à vendre un assortiment très complet de livres de comptes de différentes grandeurs et de différentes qualités, livres d'Eglise, livres pour les écoles, et une variété d'autres, qu'il offre en vente en gros et en détail à des prix très-modérés.

                        JOHN CAMPBELL.

Montréal, 29 Sept. 1827.—Q-I.

Left: Advertisement in the Bytown Gazette, *September 27, 1837; Advertisement in* La Minerve, *October 1, 1827.*
National Library of Canada, NL-22096; NL-22105

A letter from Duncan Finlayson to the Gentlemen in Charge of Posts in a communication to the Red River Settlement, May 25, 1846, to be dispatched "with all possible haste." The log of the letter's itinerary shows that it went via the east-west route, which lay entirely north of the US border. The letter reached the Red River settlement nearly six weeks later, on July 12. In light of such lengthy delays, mail more commonly travelled to the Red River Settlement via the north-south route that went by cart, dogsled or steamboat through the United States to St. Paul and then north through Pembina, in what is now North Dakota. Hudson's Bay Company Archives, Provincial Archives of Manitoba, HBCA B.235/c/1 fo. 133 (N14640)

A cover from the colonial period on a letter scale. After January 5, 1844, the postage on all letters and newspapers handled by the colonial mails was assessed by weight; previously, a postage fee was levied for each single sheet. The new system was adopted partly in response to public pressure; according to a commission of enquiry in the early 1840s, "the taxing of letters by weight seems to be desired by the inhabitants of these colonies. . . . Mercantile men and other persons, whose views are most entitled to consideration, advocate with great unanimity, the adoption of the English system." CPM 1983.192.12.2, 1994.118.2 (CD)

THE COLONIAL ERA

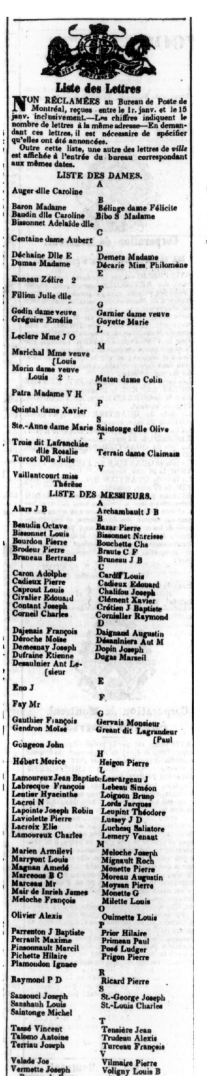

POST-OFFICE, MONTREAL, CANADA.

The colonial press and the postal system were inseparable if reluctant bedfellows. The press provided postal officials with access to the public. Announcements, transport contracts and post office schedules were publicized via newspaper advertisements. Postal officials used newspapers to attack their opponents and defend their actions. Similarly, the press relied on the post for the free mailing of single copies of newspapers between publishers. Yesterday's headlines in Toronto could become tomorrow's copy in Quebec City. The mail was also the publisher's lifeline to his customers; however, the postal service demanded payment in advance. This was an ongoing source of contention between the press and the postal authority.

From the perspective of the newspaper publishers, prepaid postage added to their cost of doing business. A more equitable practice, in their view, would be for the subscribers to pay the postage, but the Deputy Postmaster General at that time, Thomas Allen Stayner, refused to endorse this policy. Instead, he

Top: Post-Office, Montreal, Canada, 1857. *During the 1850s, the governments of Canada West and Canada East built substantial post offices in Toronto, Kingston and Montreal. The first stone of this building was laid in 1853. The wood engraving is attributed to Kilburn.* McCord Museum of Canadian History, Montreal, M 985.230.5877.3

Left: This list of unclaimed letters at the Montreal Post Office was published in La Minerve *on January 23, 1855. At the time, there was no such thing as free home delivery.* National Library of Canada, NL-22110

Both sides of a letter addressed to Joseph Masson, February 6, 1840. This letter travelled through the postal system to Liverpool, probably via New York. Archives nationales du Québec à Montréal, Fonds Succession Joseph Masson P313 (1990-10-060\35)

MAIL CONTRACT.

Any persons desirous of entering into a contract for the conveyance of the Mails between

Fredericton & St. Stephens, OR Fredericton & St. Andrews,

once per week each way, commencing from the 10th May next, or as much earlier as possible, are requested to send in Sealed Tenders, addressed to the Postmaster General, stating the sum per annum for which they will agree to perform the service.

Tenders will be received at the same time for the performance of the above service twice per week each way.

Tenders will be received until Saturday the 3d April next at noon; each Tender to be accompanied with the names of two responsible persons to become bound with the party tendering for the due and faithful performance of the service.

The Mails to be conveyed on such days and at such hours, as may from time to time be appointed by the Postmaster General.

N.B. It is to be distinctly understood that persons tendering for the above service will have no claim whatever upon the Legislature for any, the smallest remuneration, over and above the amount named in the Tender.

J. HOWE, P. M. G.

General Post Office,
St. John, March 16, 1852.

An 1852 call for tenders from New Brunswick stagecoach entrepreneurs. Provincial Archives of New Brunswick, RS 121 J 5

charged a tax of up to five shillings per newspaper mailed to subscribers. The resulting revenue went directly into his salary. It was not used to run the post office, a point made repeatedly and forcefully by irate newspaper publishers.

Throughout the 1840s, prominent businessmen and politicians in British North America argued strongly in favour of postal reform. They called for cheaper postage and repatriation of the postal system. Postal reform soon became part of the demand for greater domestic control over colonial affairs, and, when Responsible Government was granted in 1848, reform of the postal system and its devolution to the colonial legislatures came with it. The symbol of this devolution was the creation, in 1851, of a postage stamp for each of the provinces of Canada, New Brunswick and Nova Scotia. After more than two centuries, an independent Canadian postal system was gradually emerging from the shadow of imperial control.

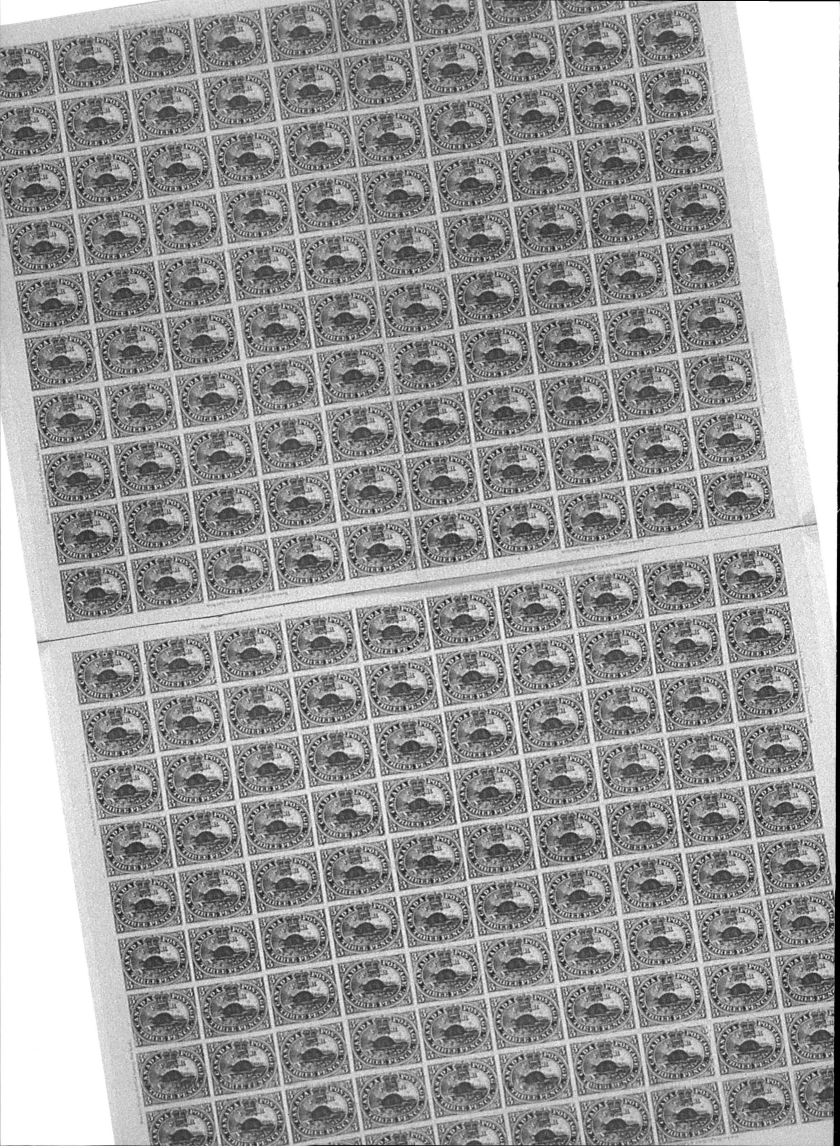

POSTAGE STAMPS:
WINDOWS *on the* WORLD

Chantal Amyot

Until the middle of the nineteenth century, mailing costs were paid by recipients and calculated on the basis of distance. In England, in 1837, a schoolmaster by the name of Rowland Hill became an advocate of postal reform. He suggested that the sender be responsible for postal charges, and that these should be based on weight. In August, 1839, Queen Victoria ratified the bill on postal reform, which stipulated that a standard tax of one penny must be paid in advance by the sender of any piece of mail sent anywhere in British territory. As proof that the tax had actually been paid and to avoid fraud, Rowland Hill proposed that a small square of adhesive paper be attached to each letter. His proposal was implemented in 1840, and Mr. Hill became known as Sir Rowland Hill when he was knighted by the Queen in 1860. Between 1839, when the reform was passed, and 1840, when the first postage stamp was released, postal authorities continued to use the old system, which was not very practical: an ink inscription on the cover showed that postage had been paid.

The first postage stamp in the world, the "Penny Black," issued in 1840, bore a picture of Queen Victoria, and it also gave rise to the expression "penny post":

> Of all the posts, the penny post
> Is that in which I delight the most,
> Since now my letters, few or many,
> Come with the friendly pre-paid penny.
> So, be they full of wit or phlegm,
> My only tax is reading them.

In 1840, England issued the Penny Black, the first postage stamp in the world. Ever since, this country has had the exclusive privilege of not having to mark its name on stamps; the profile of the monarch suffices to indicate the stamp's origin. By permission of the British Library. The Penny Black Stamp is a registered trade mark of the British Post Office. Reproduced by kind permission of the British Post Office.

Facing page: Plate proof sheet of two hundred Three Pence Beaver stamps. NAC/POS-003600

Thus, housemaids now can send their letters
As free and frankly as their betters;
And waft a sigh, in strains of Pindus,
From kitchen fires as far as Indus
Or launch their passion hot as coals,
To warm their lovers at the Poles,
All hail, then penny-letter trade,
(The best reform the Whigs have made,)
Whose flakey showers, like March-tide-bail,
O'erspread the earth by every mail.
— Philo-Denarius, *Bytown Gazette*, May 28, 1840

A page of Sir Sandford Fleming's diary. Private collection. Reproduced on the cover of *The Sandford Fleming Three Pence Essay,* Charles G. Firby Auctions (Waterford, 1996).

The colonies and other countries gradually adopted the system of postage stamps that is still used today around the world. At first, stamps were printed on large sheets and cut apart with scissors. In Canada, the perforated edges that we associate with postage stamps — so characteristic and practical — first appeared in 1858 on the halfpenny stamp. Since then, perforations have been used exclusively, except for some recent issues of self-adhesive stamps.

Everything Began with a Beaver

"Monday, February 24, 1851. Breakfasted at Ellahs [sic] Hotel with Mr. Rutter & Hon'ble Js Morris, Post Master General. Designing postage stamps for him." Great Britain had just turned over the responsibility of colonial post offices to the provinces of British North America, and this brief entry in the diary of Sir Sandford Fleming, a civil engineer and an important figure in Canadian history, marked the beginning of the history of Canadian postage stamps.

For this first Canadian stamp, Sir Sandford suggested the picture of a beaver, saying that the animal was a symbol of the industry and economy of our land and people, and that the beaver was known for its hard work, as were Canadians. His choice marked a departure from the then current practice (only about ten years old, we should remember) of representing the head of state on stamps; Queen Victoria had appeared on British and colonial stamps up until that time. On April 23, 1851, the Province of Canada released its Three Pence Beaver.

As well as creating the first three Canadian postage stamps, Sir Sandford Fleming (1827-1915) was the chief engineer of the Intercolonial Railway and the Canadian Pacific Railway. He was also responsible for the adoption of international standard time and the division of the globe into time zones. This bust is the work of sculptor Hamilton T.C.P. MacCarthy (1907). CPM 1974.2135.1. (CD)

Snuffbox belonging to the Fleming family. CPM 1989.1.1 (CD)

The Half cent Black of the Large Queen issues, released in April, 1868, was actually the first postage stamp of the Dominion of Canada, created in 1867 by the British North America Act, but philatelists consider the Three Pence Beaver of 1851 the first Canadian stamp. Today it is a prestigious collector's item, in spite of contemporary opinion of its merits. An item in the *Montreal Gazette* on May 5, 1851, says, "The postage stamps have been received; and, Mr. Porteous has them for sale at the Post Office, but only those of the denomination of 3d. They are coarsely and wretchedly executed. It was little worth while to send to New York for such workmanship; and, we rather suspect Mr. Morris will not employ the same engravers again."

Less than a month after the introduction of the Three Pence Beaver, the Six Pence Consort appeared on May 17, 1851. This time, Sir Sandford chose to depict Prince Albert, husband of the Queen. Then came the Twelve Pence Black, on June 14, 1851, reproducing a portrait of Queen Victoria by A.E. Chalon. A copy of this painting had decorated a wall in the Legislative Assembly in Montreal. On April 25, 1849, Sir Sandford had found himself there when, after a series of riots, fire destroyed the Assembly buildings. He had rushed out with the painting, and, once beyond danger, he had cut the canvas

Facing page: Stamp boxes made their appearance shortly after stamps were introduced; their popularity reached a peak in the period between 1890 and World War I. CPM (CD)

Corner pair of the Twelve Pence Black in mint condition. Of the 51,000 items printed, only 1450 were sold; the remaining 49,550 were destroyed.
NAC/POS-000031

away to get rid of the heavy frame. He kept the rolled canvas in his studio under his desk, and, two years later, he used it to create his Twelve Pence Black stamp. Once the stamp was issued, Postmaster General James Morris asked Fleming to return the painting to its rightful place with the government. Although the Twelve Pence Black is not the rarest Canadian stamp, it is one of the better-known.

In the Other Colonies of British North America
Before joining Confederation, one after another, the colonies of New Brunswick, Nova Scotia, British Columbia, Vancouver Island, Prince Edward Island and Newfoundland produced their own postage stamps. In February 1851, the Lieutenant-Governor of Nova Scotia, Sir Edmund Head, proposed that all British North American colonies use the same postage stamp, the different names of the colonies being the only distinguishing feature. His motion was rejected, but Nova Scotia and New Brunswick did join together to issue a series of postage stamps with the same design in September 1851.

In 1857, Newfoundland issued its first postage stamps. This colony was the only one in British North America at the time to make stamps triangular in shape and to use a different stamp for each postal rate.

In 1860, the colonies of British Columbia and Vancouver Island jointly released a postage stamp, but, five years later, they returned to separate designs. Joined in a single territory on November 19, 1866, they nonetheless used different stamps until 1871. Between 1861 and 1873, Prince Edward Island used its own postage stamps; all sixteen issues from this period bore the picture of Queen Victoria.

Portrait of Her Majesty Queen Victoria by Alfred Edward Chalon.
NAC/C-041148

Joint issue, Vancouver Island and British Columbia, 1860.
NAC/POS-001258

First Newfoundland stamp issue, 1857. CPM (SD)

First New Brunswick stamp issue, 1851, cancelled. CPM (SD)

Fifth Prince Edward Island stamp issue, 1862. CPM (SD)

Christmas Stamps: A World Premiere

In 1898, Postmaster General Sir William Mulock proposed a new rate system that would allow one to send a letter anywhere in the British Empire for the fixed sum of two cents. To launch this Imperial Post, Sir William chose as a design for the first stamp a map of the world on which the territories of the British Empire were shown in red.

At this time, every new stamp had to be approved by Queen Victoria. When the Postmaster General of Great Britain, the Duke of Norfolk, presented her with the model of this one, the Queen asked for the issue date. The Duke replied that the new stamp was to come out on the prince's birthday. Queen Victoria asked, "Which prince do you mean?" The Duke replied, "The Prince of Peace, Ma'am."

So it was that on December 25, 1898, the Imperial Post was established and Canada became the first country in the world to issue a Christmas stamp, inscribed "XMAS 1898." A second inscription underneath reads: "We hold a vaster Empire than has been," a phrase taken from a song composed by Sir Lewis Morris in 1887 to celebrate Queen Victoria's Golden Jubilee:

> We hold a vaster Empire than has been!
> Nigh half the race of man is subject to our Queen!
> Nigh half the wide, wide earth is ours in fee!
> And where her rule comes, all are free.
> And therefore 'tis, oh Queen, that we,
> Knit fast in bonds of temperate liberty,
> Rejoice today, and make our solemn jubilee!

The December 1898 issue marked the beginnings of the Imperial Post. CPM (SD)

Twenty million Christmas stamps had been ordered, ten million with a lavender-coloured ocean and ten million with a blue ocean. The complexity of the design and the multiplicity of colours used for this postage stamp caused numerous variations in the lots that were printed. There are also a number of errors in the tone of the red that represented the British territories, somewhat modifying the boundaries of the Empire.

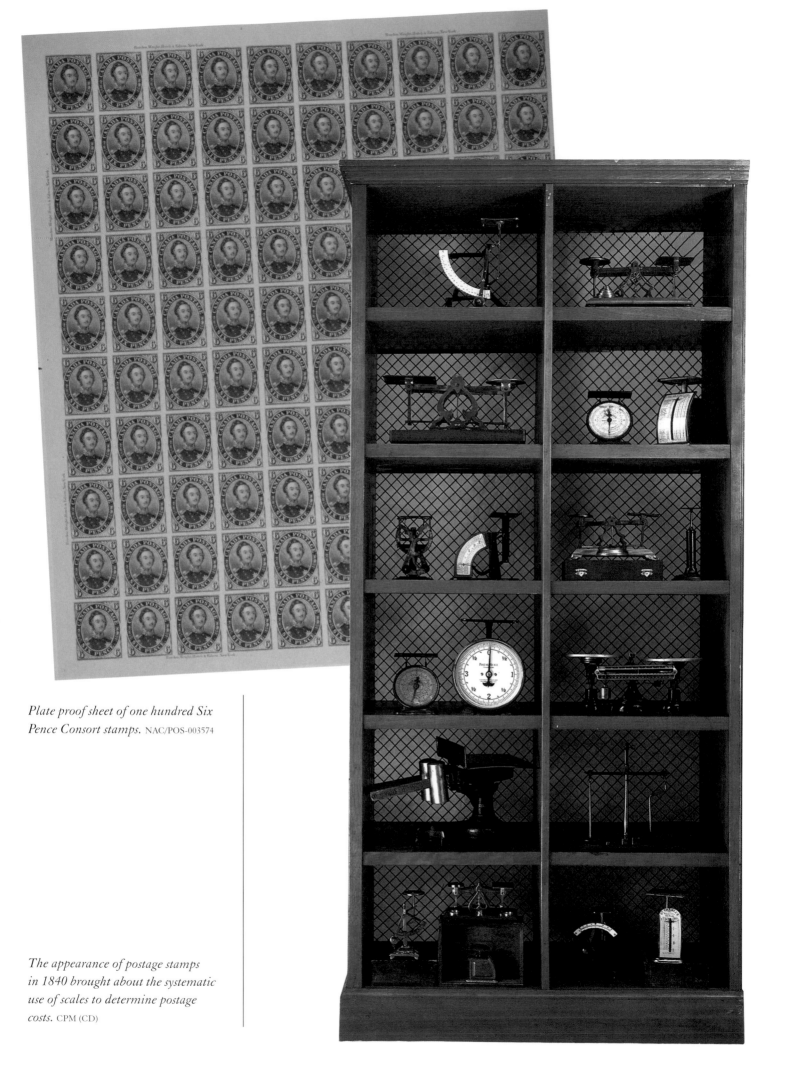

Plate proof sheet of one hundred Six Pence Consort stamps. NAC/POS-003574

The appearance of postage stamps in 1840 brought about the systematic use of scales to determine postage costs. CPM (CD)

In less than a hundred and fifty years, more than two thousand different designs of postage stamps have been issued in Canada, with an impressive range of themes, including the reigning monarch, winter sports, the achievements of Canadian astronauts, flora and fauna, aboriginal life and art, masterpieces of Canadian painting, Superman and Christmas — making more than two thousand little windows on the world, through which others can view the richness and variety of Canadian culture.

Montage of objects in memory of Sir William Mulock, including a photograph taken at the 1898 conference in London at which the principle of the Imperial Post was adopted. CPM (CD)

This double-sided brass clock was suspended above the elevator doors in the main foyer of the Besserer Street post office in Ottawa. CPM 1974.2165.5 (CD)

THE POST OFFICE:
AT THE HEART *of the* NATION

Chantal Amyot

Today, postal business can be carried out in buildings specifically designed for this purpose and in a variety of local businesses that include a postal franchise. Rather than the architectural design of the building, it is the Canada Post logo that allows the public to identify the availability of postal services on sites spreading right into cyberspace, where Canada Post Internet has staked out new territory. For many years, however, the very presence of a post office was an asset of great importance to the community.

In a territory as vast and sparsely populated as Canada, a dependable postal distribution system is a serious challenge. At the end of the nineteenth century, this system evolved in step with the railway system, and both contributed to pushing back the country's borders and developing the land. During this period, the establishment of a post office had the effect of anchoring a town or village in the communication and business networks, and it also symbolized the hope, prosperity and stability of the muni cipality to which it belonged.

Several factors came into play when a community tried to justify the establishment of a post office, but there was one that made all the difference: it had to be near a train station. As the railway system expanded, community development was almost entirely dependent on the route taken by the railroad, particularly in western Canada. A train station was practically a necessity for a town's growth. In Manitoba, the municipality of Millford went so far as to pick up and move — houses, businesses, hotels and all — to get closer to the new station in Glenboro. The community also had to be able to offer a strategic location for its post office, so that there was easy public access as well as an efficient means of transferring the mail between the post office and the wider transportation network.

The post office in Montague, Prince Edward Island, constructed in 1888.
NAC/POS-002912

Facing page: (top) The post office in Thetford Mines, Quebec, which opened in 1939. Its Art Deco curves reflect the tastes of the times. (CD) *(inset bottom left) The Vancouver post office and mail processing plant, built according to the plans of McCarter and Nairne, opened in 1958.* (LG)

Below: The post office in Dawson, Yukon, built in 1901 according to the plans of Thomas Fuller. NAC/PA-067219

Above: The post office in Chester, Nova Scotia, built in 1939-1940, stands at the corner of Queen and Union streets. (JS)

Below: The post office in Wolf Creek, Alberta, built in 1910, as it appeared in 1913. NAC/PA-017480 (H. Matheson)

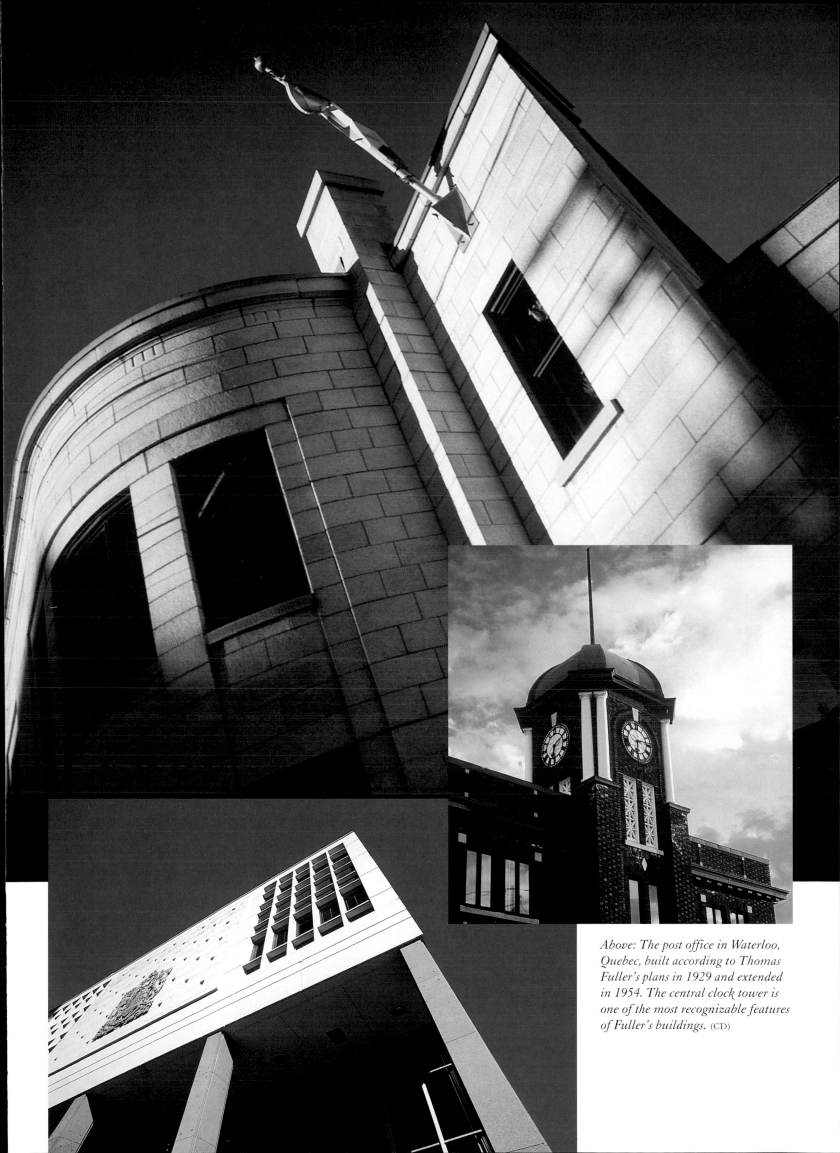

Above: The post office in Waterloo, Quebec, built according to Thomas Fuller's plans in 1929 and extended in 1954. The central clock tower is one of the most recognizable features of Fuller's buildings. (CD)

These bronze plaques were among the lavish interior decorations of the Besserer Street post office, Ottawa, which opened its doors on November 11, 1936. Designed by Cecil Burgess under the direction of architect and designer Edward Gardner, this seven-storey building became the main post office of the national capital. Postal services, including mailing, handling and sorting, could all be carried out here, and its ideal location near Union Station made shipping and receiving mail easy. The bronze plaques shown here represent eight of the ten Canadian postage stamps which Gardner selected from his private collection. When the building was demolished in 1981 during the redevelopment of downtown Ottawa, the Canadian Postal Museum acquired many of its beautiful and interesting artifacts. CPM (CD)

Design detail of the façade of the Ottawa post office station B, officially opened in November, 1939, by the Right Honourable W. L. Mackenzie King. (SD)

The choice of materials to be used for the construction of a post office was an important consideration: if they were costly, the town would appear to be rich and prosperous. Humboldt, a small town in Saskatchewan, saw its status change in everyone's eyes from the moment that a red brick post office was built there. If the government was willing to invest so noticeably in a town, it must be a going concern!

The interiors of post offices were always neat and pleasant, and more or less ornate depending on the size of the community and the prosperity of the region. The public area — generally a third of the space — contained tables, counters, bulletin boards, lock boxes and a portrait of the reigning monarch. The work space, rarely visible to the public, contained all the apparatus necessary to handle and sort the mail.

As Chief Architect for the Department of Public Works, Thomas Fuller was responsible for the construction of government buildings across Canada, notably the Parliament Buildings in Ottawa; it's no wonder that there is a striking similarity between the architecture of the Parliament Buildings and that of post offices. Except for their very different scale, they show numerous common features. The most evident are their Second-Empire-style symmetry and mansard roofs, as well as the flowing, elongated details

Located at the corner of Buade and Du Fort streets, the Quebec City post office was built in 1872 according to plans by architect Pierre Gauvreau, under the direction of chief architect T.S. Scott. When it was renovated and extended between 1913 and 1919, under the direction of chief architect David Edwart, some of the original Second Empire details were eliminated in favour of Beaux-Arts elements, and the mansard roof was replaced by a flat one. (CD)

Brass lock boxes bearing the royal initials VR (Victoria Regina). CPM 1974.2133.1 (CD)

At the Vancouver post office, 1999. (LG)

typical of the Victorian Gothic style, including pointed windows, multiple levels, towers and many sculptural details. A tower was often the predominant feature of Fuller's post offices, and the tower of the Centre Block of the Parliament Buildings is one of its most striking elements. It follows, then, that the similarity in form reinforces the presence of the government symbolized in its buildings across the country.

An Important Link

At the end of the nineteenth century the country was developing rapidly, and, after 1882, considerable funds were allocated by the Department of Public Works to improve the quantity and quality of public buildings across Canada. New federal buildings were needed for the new provinces, and the more the provinces developed the more services were needed to consolidate the growing country.

The post office served as a concrete sign of the federal government's presence across the land. In rural areas, it became an indispensable link between the general population and the national capital. It was the place where people could find the forms required for government services and where they could speak to a representative of the government, the postmaster. Henri Roy, who worked in the post office at Sainte-Anne-des-Monts, Quebec, for more than fifty years — first for his father, and then as postmaster himself — remembers filling out official forms for clients over the years; some of these people could not read or

The post office in Mission City, British Columbia, built in 1935 and renovated in 1955. (LG)

write, but others simply thought that the postmaster would be better able to perform the administrative tasks required by the government. In many cases, post offices housed other governmental services, including customs, weights and measures, and internal revenue.

Post office boxes from the end of the nineteenth century, with brass doors decorated with beaver designs. CPM 1991.37.1 (CD)

Because of the fundamental role they played in communities, the number of post offices grew rapidly. Between 1871 and 1891, their number doubled, from 3943 to 8041. In 1911, there were 13,324 post offices across Canada.

Although many post offices were the work of Fuller or were inspired by Fuller's designs, most of those in small communities were not. In rural and semi-rural areas at the beginning of the twentieth century, many municipalities had their own post offices, which blended into the architectural style of the rest of the town. Often these post offices were situated in small stores, such as the general store or the drug store, or even in private homes, and thus they were as varied in style as the range of Canadian domestic architecture would allow. What is surprising, perhaps, is that today we have come full circle: the link between local businesses and the post office has been re-established nearly a century later.

Inside the Vancouver post office. (LG)

THE RURAL POSTMASTER

John Willis

In the cities and small towns across Canada, the post office was a tangible symbol of federal grandeur. In the smaller rural communities, however, it took on a different shape and significance. Here, the post office was a centre of daily life, where the postmaster, entrusted with the written correspondence of the inhabitants, processed their outgoing mail and distributed their incoming letters, parcels and newspapers. The rural post office also served as a kind of community centre, where people met their neighbours, exchanged information, and took a break from their labours.

The postmasters were the hosts of these community centres. They handled the mail and sometimes even their patrons' money, and they also might dispense advice and help out with some of the necessities of life. Theirs was a unique social position in the rural landscape of Canada, at once belonging to and set apart from the community.

The Outgoing Mail

In the winter, the post office woodstove would crackle, warming the ink as well as the air. The ink was the lifeblood of the post office. Every article of mail leaving the post office had to be stamped with the day's date and either AM or PM to indicate whether it was in the morning or the afternoon post. In order to get a clear, readable impression, the postmaster would insert a rubber pad beneath each envelope before striking the letter with his cancellation hammer, creating the muted thumping sound so characteristic of the post office.

The postmaster and his wife outside the Cheam View, British Columbia, post office, around 1928. Cecil C. Coutts, *Cancelled with Pride: A History of Chilliwack Area Post Offices 1865-1993* (Cecil C. Coutts Publishing, 1993)

Facing page: The postmaster's drawer: stickers and coupons used in processing the mail. CPM (CD)

Wire cord, sealer, and lead used to fasten and secure a mailbag. The mouth of the mailbag is fastened shut by pulling the wire cord through the grommets. The cord ends are threaded through the openings in a lead nugget or plug, which resembles a small sinker for a fishing line. The sealer, a tool similar to pliers, is used to squeeze the nugget firmly onto the cord so that no mail can escape from the bag and no one can tamper with the mail. CPM (CD)

The desk and wicket used by a former postmaster of Woodford, Ontario. CPM 1981.31.1 (CD)

The postmaster stacked the letters with the stamp in the upper right hand corner, then sorted them according to destination. Many built their own furniture for sorting. The Val Morin Station post office was equipped with a homemade sorting case with sixteen pigeonholes. Half of them held letters for various destinations, and the others served as convenient parking spots for the various forms and letter bills that would accompany the packets of letters. At the Trappist monastery in Oka, Quebec, the postmaster and his assistants built a beautiful revolving sorting case. The postmaster would bind or "tie out" the letters into packages of not more than about seventy-five, cutting lengths of twine with a small curved knife on a ring which he wore on his finger.

Letter packages were sorted into canvas bags strung on wooden or metal racks. Processing parcels was more work than tying out letters, and it could keep the postmaster busy for hours. Each parcel had to be weighed, since parcel post rates varied according to weight. Poorly packed parcels would have to be rewrapped, and sometimes the contents would spill out on the floor, much to the dismay of the postmaster, especially if they gave off a pungent odour. Nevertheless, customers insisted that their freshly baked cakes or their favourite fresh fish be delivered on time and intact.

Waiting for the Mail

In a small community, the arrival of the mail was an important daily ritual. It could bring news or, better still, money from a far-away family member, an anxiously awaited message from a business partner in a distant city, or a daily or weekly newspaper. Or maybe the long-awaited cream separator or sewing machine would finally arrive from one of the mail order companies — Eaton's, Simpson's or Dupuis Frères. Whatever the item, rural residents were highly dependent on the postmaster to sort the incoming mail quickly.

Mail sorting case from the Trappist monastery in Oka, Quebec. There are pigeonholes on all four sides, which can be accessed by turning the entire case. The bottom surfaces of the pigeonholes are worn from repeated friction of paper and hands. CPM 1990.35.1 (CD)

This money bag for transporting cash was used by Leroy Kuan, president of the Canadian Postmasters and Assistants Association, when he was postmaster of Cabri, Saskatchewan. The envelopes and forms of the Post Office Savings Bank were sent to Ottawa by the postmaster.
CPM (CD)

SPRING CHICKENS

"There was always a time each spring when you could hear chickens cackling away in the mailroom at the post office. We received 10, 15, 20, 25 or 30 boxes at a time, and each one contained about 100 or 125 chickens. . . . When they arrived, we phoned the recipients as soon as possible so that they would come and get them. Often, we couldn't reach people; they weren't there. The noise went on all day and all night. We did everything we could to deliver them. . . . Sometimes we looked after them by feeding them grain, some sort of bran, especially if they stayed more than a day or two. And sometimes we saw dead ones through the holes in the boxes."
— *Victorien Naud,*
retired postmaster, Barraute,
Quebec, March 1990

Mildred Roylance, a former postmistress in Greenwood, British Columbia, would awake very early, sort the mail, and return home to have breakfast before her regular opening time. When mail arrived during the day, she had to shut down the wicket temporarily while she sorted it, a task that could take anywhere from thirty minutes to an hour or more, depending on the volume of mail and the number of hands available to do the work. Around 1895, the postmaster in the coal mining town of Union (now Cumberland) on Vancouver Island was assisted by the cashier of a nearby store and the paymaster of the Union Colliery Company. Both were definite assets to the postmaster because between them they knew most of the people to whom the mail was addressed.

When the mail was not sorted promptly enough for the customers, there was hell to pay. One evening in 1898, the Reverend Louis Poitras paced furiously for three hours up and down outside the post office in Nelson, British Columbia. "This is true tyranny," he wrote in a letter to the Postmaster General. "We have always received our letters and papers one half hour after the arrival of the trains, why do we not have the same justice today?" For Poitras, the quicker he got his important and pressing letters, the quicker he could write the answers that needed to go out in the next morning's mail. For him, as for many, the speed of the mail was of utmost importance.

The mail was distributed to post office patrons by general delivery at the wicket, or it was put into lock boxes. At Val Morin Station, as in most post offices, general delivery letters were arranged in alphabetical order in a case that hung from the wall to the left of the wicket interior, easily accessible when customers came by to pick up their mail. Some customers, usually the more affluent ones, preferred to pick up their mail from private lock boxes to which only the postmaster and the patron had the key or combination. Some of these were utilitarian in appearance, but some were of elaborate design, with beautiful patterns of metal, wood and glass.

Above: The postmistress of Cressman, Saskatchewan, in the doorway of the post office, awaiting the mail with her customers and their horses.
Saskatchewan Archives Board, Photo S-B 1429

Top: Rural mailboxes in a landscape of ice and snow. (CD)

Rural mail delivery began in 1908. Couriers operating out of local post offices deposited mail in mailboxes set up beside the road, and they also picked up the outgoing mail that customers left in the mailboxes. When people wanted to mail parcels, they might leave cash for the postage and expect the courier to return their change with the next delivery. Originally, the couriers did their work on horseback or perhaps from a buggy in summer and a sleigh in winter, but they began to use automobiles when enough roads had been built. Rural mail carriers still use their cars to bring postal services to their neighbours.

Beyond the Call of Duty

The intimacy of the rural post office made it a place where people who lived miles apart gathered to exchange pleasantries with distant neighbours and to confide in the postmaster. At the post office in East Advocate, Nova Scotia, the postmistress's husband built a drop box with a window in the outside of the house. None of the patrons ever bothered to use it because they much preferred to step inside and have a chat with the postmistress. When she became aware of this, she began to store her knitting inside the box. In

Above: The postmaster, J.W. Cooke, and his two assistants, Cumberland, British Columbia, around 1915.
C30.1, Cumberland Museum & Archives

Inset, top right: A customer collects his daily paper from the post office in Merrickville, Ontario, 1947.
NAC/C-053550 (Wilfred Doucette)

Right: Mail time at the post office in Lloydminster, Saskatchewan, in the early 1920s. Barr Colony Heritage Cultural Centre, Lloydminster Alberta/Saskatchewan

Craiglands, Saskatchewan, people picking up their mail at the post office often stayed for tea and cookies. One family would come for the mail on Fridays and spend the entire evening listening to the radio with the postmaster and his family.

The rural postmaster was usually a trusted and respected member of the community to whom residents could turn for help or small favours. In the Tenescape, Nova Scotia, postal ledgers are hand-written notes to the postmistress, dating from the turn of the twentieth century, politely asking her to pass their letters on to other customers. In 1939, one Alberta postmaster reported, "I list about twenty pensioners as the finest patrons of this office. Each first of the month I see them all; they wouldn't dream of asking anyone else to witness their signatures or help them to fill in their pension documents."

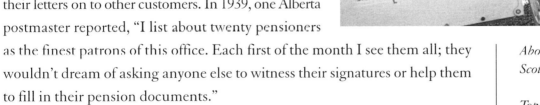

Above: Rural mail delivery in Nova Scotia. (JS)

Top: Rural mailboxes on a country road in the Eastern Townships, Quebec. (CD)

The rural postmaster sometimes took on the role of village confessor. At Sainte-Anne-des-Monts, Quebec, a man with three daughters confided to the postmaster, Henri Roy, that the parish priest believed his daughters were pregnant and should be dismissed from their jobs as school teachers. M. Roy advised the distraught father that if he let some time pass the priest would be proven wrong. He was. The same postmaster was approached regularly to write love letters, and, in some cases, he penned both sides of the amorous correspondence.

One special category of mail going through the hands of the postmaster was money. In the absence of a reliable express system, banks and other institutions transferred large amounts of cash in special bags through the post. Individuals and businesses could (and still can) move money around the country in the

The postmaster put patrons' mail into the lock boxes from the back, behind the wicket, and they used their keys to open the boxes and retrieve it from the public area in front of the wicket. This piece of wicket furniture contains seventy-six glass-faced boxes, a row of fourteen wood-faced ones along the bottom, and one double box just beneath the wicket.
CPM 1974.2168.1 (CD)

form of postal money orders. From 1868 to 1969, Canadians could save money at the Post Office Savings Bank, a headquarters banking system. Deposits and withdrawals were made at local branches, the postmaster serving as a liaison between customers and the head office in Ottawa. A good deal of trust was thus invested in the postmaster; such transactions were serious affairs.

Postmaster and Patrons in Conflict

At times, relations between the postmaster and the public became strained. Given the important and respected role of the postmaster, these were unusual and unsettling occasions, but sometimes postmasters were forced to stand apart from their communities. In 1920, for example, when Canada was in the throes of an anti-Bolshevik panic, the criminal code was amended to make preaching the violent overthrow of the government illegal. A circular was distributed to all the postmasters asking them to be on the lookout for potentially subversive mail, thus making spies of them:

> Postmasters are instructed that in the event of their observing
> publications passing through the mails which, in their opinion,
> contravene the above sections of the Criminal Code, specimen
> copies, together with such particulars as are available as to the
> origins, quantity and destination of the matter, are to be
> forwarded by first mail under cover to the Postmaster General,
> Ottawa.

The postmistress puts up a movie poster in Sainte-Adèle, Quebec. The post office was a bulletin board for community announcements as well as a conduit for government information. NAC/PA-169765 (John F. Mailer)

Receipt for registered mail. CPM 1974.1953.16. (CD)

Postmasters were frequently at odds with their customers over post office hours. After World War II, the postmaster of Coronation, Alberta, changed the closing time at his post office from eight p.m. to six p.m. He realized that his patrons were not amused when he walked into the local bar and a hush fell over the entire room. During the 1930s and 1940s, the Quebec chapter of the Canadian Postmasters and Assistants Association fought the public and the government tooth and nail over whether post offices could close on Sundays. The postmasters wanted the day off, but they faced strenuous opposition from village and small-town patrons who wanted to continue the tradition of keeping the post office open before and after mass. In the end, the postmasters had their way, although their success may have come at some cost to their public image.

Social distance was another potential source of discord between postmasters and patrons. Economic and racial differences, sometimes unspoken, disturbed the normally amicable relations between them. In Ignace, Ontario, a postmaster's wife was known as the Duchess, in keeping with her status as the wife of the owner of the general store and a hotel. Canadian Pacific Railway foreman F.B. Docks and his wife ran the post office in the Iroquois village of

This sign separated the public areas from the post office work area, marking a clear boundary between official government business and the convivial everyday life of the village. CPM 1993.16.114 (Harry Foster)

CHEZ OUELLETTE: THE POST OFFICE AT VAL MORIN STATION, 1914-1983

The post office of Val Morin Station, Quebec, was located a short distance from the railway track. It was a capacious structure built around 1910 by Fidèle Ouellette, a handyman and mechanic. In addition to the post office, Fidèle and Corinne, his wife, kept a general store and took in summer boarders.

The post office was actually run by Corinne Ouellette, the assistant postmistress, and she was succeeded by her daughters, Monique and Félicitée, in 1941. A constant stream of visitors kept the sisters busy behind the wicket, especially in the summer, when the line of customers might extend through the store and out into the street.

The post office closed in 1983, although Félicitée and her husband, Lucien Lepage, pictured above in 1993, continued to operate the general store. In 1993, the complete interior of the post office and its contents were acquired by the Canadian Postal Museum, where artifacts from it are on display.

Above: Lucien Lepage and Félicitée Ouellette behind the counter of the Val Morin Station general store in 1993. (SD)

Right: Cash register. CPM 1993.16.27.1 (CD)
Postcards depicting the area around the village of Val Morin Station, Quebec. CPM

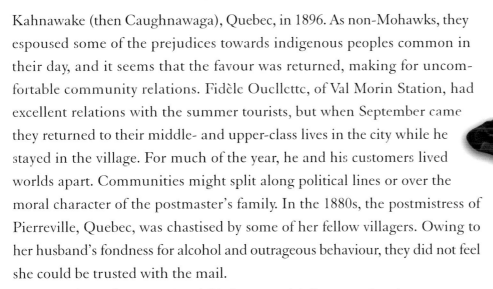

Kahnawake (then Caughnawaga), Quebec, in 1896. As non-Mohawks, they espoused some of the prejudices towards indigenous peoples common in their day, and it seems that the favour was returned, making for uncomfortable community relations. Fidèle Ouellette, of Val Morin Station, had excellent relations with the summer tourists, but when September came they returned to their middle- and upper-class lives in the city while he stayed in the village. For much of the year, he and his customers lived worlds apart. Communities might split along political lines or over the moral character of the postmaster's family. In the 1880s, the postmistress of Pierreville, Quebec, was chastised by some of her fellow villagers. Owing to her husband's fondness for alcohol and outrageous behaviour, they did not feel she could be trusted with the mail.

Notwithstanding occasional friction or social discrepancies, the postmaster was an integral part of a society in which a visit to the post office was no less important than attending church on Sunday or walking down Main Street. Under these circumstances, the contributions of rural postmasters and postmistresses were significant. They imparted a human face to the Post Office Department; they were attentive to the various needs of their customers; and they enabled their patrons to stay in touch with the wider world. Indeed, they are still a vital part of the rural postal service.

Above: Spring scale used to weigh outgoing mail. CPM 1976.14.1 (CD)

Top: Henri Roy, the postmaster of Sainte-Anne-des-Monts, Quebec, in his office, spring 1931. In addition to counselling his customers, Roy was very active in the Quebec chapter of the Canadian Postmasters and Assistants Association. Private collection

CANADIAN TIRE
CORPORATION
TORONTO-CANADA LTD.
SPRING and SUMMER-1940

THE CATALOGUE:
A DREAM INVENTORY

Chantal Amyot

Catalogue shopping has seen a century of great fluctuation. In its early days, from near the end of the nineteenth century into the 1920s, sales increased at an amazing rate. But when good roads and convenient means of transportation enabled consumers to be more mobile, and when local businesses multiplied, the popularity of mail order decreased. Today, catalogues have regained their place in the North American market: more than twelve billion are delivered annually through the mail. Like the Internet, these catalogues offer consumers a simple way to shop without the complications of getting around in bad weather, fighting through crowds or discovering that an item is out of stock.

There was a time, however, when mail order was much more than one way among others to buy an item. For several decades, it was the only way for the majority of Canadians to obtain a wide variety of items, the alternative being the limited selection of goods sold by the general store and local craftsmen.

From Sapphires to Spades
The American companies Montgomery Ward and Sears Roebuck opened their catalogue sales departments in the 1870s, but Canadian companies were slower getting

Cover of the Robert Simpson Company's 1931 Spring and Summer catalogue. Glenbow Library, Calgary, Alberta. Used with permission of Sears Canada Inc.

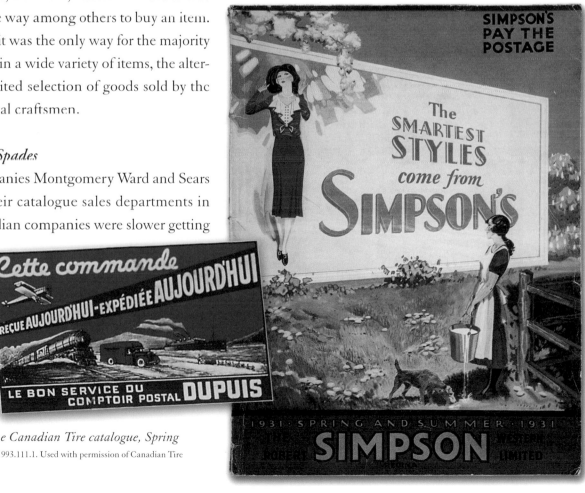

Facing page: Cover of the Canadian Tire catalogue, Spring and Summer, 1940. CPM 1993.111.1. Used with permission of Canadian Tire Corporation (CD)

Above: This advertisement for Eaton's specialized catalogues appeared in the 1931-1932 general catalogue. Glenbow Library, Calgary, Alberta. Used with permission of Sears Canada Inc.

Top right: In 1931, Dupuis Frères covered its catalogue with nationalist slogans, boasting of its French-Canadian administration and showing a statue of Dollard des Ormeaux. CPM 1997.31.5. (CD)

Right: Order form from the Dupuis Frères 1951-1952 catalogue, showing articles featuring the famous hockey player Maurice "Rocket" Richard. National Library of Canada

THE BARGAIN BOOK of A NATION!
GENERAL 1933- 1934 CATALOGUE
FALL AND WINTER
UNDERSELLING ~ DEMONSTRATION
SALE
ARMY & NAVY

EATON DU CANADA
printemps-été 1959

Pour le magasinage le plus facile
jamais fait, utilisez ce catalogue.
Il est commode, il épargne du temps, il vous
fait profiter d'un vaste choix des meilleures
offres usuelles et de la garantie EATON:
Argent remis, si la marchandise ne satisfait pas.

COMMANDEZ PAR LA POSTE
OU PAR TÉLÉPHONE
VISITEZ VOTRE BUREAU DE COMMANDES EATON

NOUS PAYONS LES FRAIS DE PORT DES COMMANDES DE $2.00 ET PLUS
TABLE DES MATIÈRES, PAGES 435-441
PLAN BUDGÉTAIRE, PAGES 432, 433

*Left: Army and Navy, owned by
British Surplus Supplies Ltd.,
opened a branch in Vancouver in
1917. The company moved its
headquarters to Regina in 1925.
Nine years later, the company started
sending over six hundred thousand
catalogues into Canadian homes
twice a year.* Toronto Public Library, Special
Collections Centre. Used with permission of Army
& Navy Department Store Limited

*Right: On the cover of the
French edition of its 1959 spring
and summer catalogue, Eaton's
offered to pay delivery charges
on orders of $2 and over.*
CPM 1993.115.2. Used with permission
of Sears Canada Inc. (CD)

Come February
We marvel at the mail.
Catalogues!
Just when we thought
Spring would never return.
Catalogues!
Promises of July
And colours in the sun.
— *Claude A. Simard,*
Painting and Planting the
Garden *(1999)*

started. Eaton's began to sell through a catalogue in 1884, and Dupuis Frères, Hudson's Bay, Morgan's and Woodward's all had a mail order service by the 1920s.

Catalogues from the beginning of the century tempted the reader with an astonishing variety of merchandise: work clothes, formal attire, jewellery, kitchen utensils, firearms, toys, medicines, tools and farm implements, musical instruments — the variety seems endless. Men, women and children could find just about anything they could possibly want or need throughout their lives.

But the most surprising item in the pages of these catalogues is, beyond a doubt, houses. In Eaton's 1912 catalogue, there are no fewer than nineteen models that can be ordered. In general, they are rather elegant two-storey country homes with between five and ten bedrooms and sometimes a veranda. Plans cost $2.50, while the supplies and materials necessary for a six-bedroom house (including a bathroom) cost about $1000. Except for bricks and stones, all of this material would be mailed to the buyer.

Three items sold by catalogue achieved unprecedented success and contributed to significant changes in the lives of the rural population at the beginning of the twentieth century. The sewing machine, which enabled the housewife to make household items and her family's clothing more efficiently; the bicycle, a recreational novelty that rapidly became a useful means of transportation; and the cream separator, which increased farm productivity by enabling cream to be separated more completely and quickly from milk.

Catalogue sales were so successful that specialized catalogues began to appear. There were catalogues for wallpaper, for books, for candy, for sewing patterns, for surveying equipment. Commercial enterprises also took into consideration the specific needs of different regions. In British Columbia,

Eaton's 1959 catalogue offered everything the farmer could wish for. Cream separators, introduced in the 1890s, were a popular catalogue item for over half a century. CPM 1993.115.2.

Woodward's advertised: "We carry a large stock of umbrellas specially adapted for use in our British Columbia climate." Dupuis Frères made sure that a wide range of religious articles was available for its French-Canadian clients, who were devout Catholics.

Advantages of the Mail

Obviously, the catalogue sales system allowed companies to adjust to public demand without having to keep all their merchandise on inventory. This way, they could offer very competitive prices.

Simpson's department store
advertised itself as "A great city
store in your home." CPM 1998.58.5.
Used with permission of Sears Canada Inc. (CD)

Below: Handstamps of mail-order
catalogue companies. CPM (CD)

These companies, located in urban centres, also benefited from the transportation systems already in place — the railway and the postal system — to deliver their merchandise. Postal money orders had been available since 1855, and parcel post had existed since 1859 in Canada East and Canada West and since 1865 in Nova Scotia and New Brunswick. Other innovations in the postal system made the work of catalogue sales companies much easier. Free delivery to each house began in rural areas in 1908 and covered almost all of the eastern part of the country by 1914, and the popular COD (cash on delivery) system was introduced in 1922.

Even if the companies had to cover postage costs and did not receive preferential rates from the post office, all of these services were extremely advantageous for them. Moreover, they did not waste any time in starting to organize Christmas banquets for postmasters to thank them for their indispensable contribution to their thriving businesses. During the Christmas period, these companies often bought full-page advertisements in *The Canadian Postmaster*, the magazine of the Canadian Postmasters and Assistants Association. In 1933, the Robert Simpson Company's message read: "We take this opportunity to thank our many friends in the Postal Service of Canada for past favours and their splendid co-operation during the past twelve months. As the year 1934 dawns, we are looking forward to another year of happy relationships with you."

It is true that the postmasters were valuable and necessary allies; their volume of work increased considerably during strong sales periods when catalogue orders would be at their peak — Easter, the back-to-school period and Christmas. Some postmasters estimate that, in the first half of the twentieth century, they handled ten parcels for every first-class letter.

Facing page: Some of the wonderful merchandise that could be ordered from the catalogue and delivered by mail: women's and children's clothing, sewing machines and other sewing needs, cleaning supplies, home furnishings, and wallpaper, complete with instructions for figuring out how much to order. CPM
(Photo of Eaton's 1933 wallpaper catalogue CPM 1993.111.2.
Used with permission of Sears Canada Inc.) (CD)

A selection of contemporary catalogues. CPM (CD)

Wish Books

Well aware of their potential customers, catalogue sales companies knew how to address their main audience — women. Since women were responsible for most of the domestic work and for buying or making most of the items they needed for their homes, they were featured on the covers and key pages of the catalogues. Instructions for ordering, for example, were often illustrated with a picture of a woman at her desk filling out the order forms or opening a package.

However, not everyone was happy that rural clients could now order goods that had, up until that point, been available only in urban centres. Local merchants, especially, were offended by the excessive competition of these new consumer giants. Others opposed catalogue shopping on what they saw as moral grounds, attacking the catalogues as sources of temptation to greed and materialism. In 1907, the priest in Lévis, Quebec, preached against "this scourge of extravagant possessions, cosmetics, automobiles, alcohol, travel and pleasures of all sorts." The Desjardins cooperative movement and the Caisses Populaires Desjardins, introduced in Quebec by Alphonse Desjardins around the turn of the century, denounced catalogue shopping and urged working people not to indulge in it. Desjardins worked hard to promote the idea of saving money, and he was therefore opposed to this new form of consumer

culture, to the idea of "regular leisure periods, compulsive spending and the morality of self-satisfaction of an apparently permissive nature."

Although it is difficult to measure the impact of such rhetoric, we know, at the very least, that catalogue buying ended up causing feelings of shame in some clients. This must have been particularly true in the small communities where the postmaster was also the owner of the general store! To respond to this unfortunate situation, companies put into place a special "incognito" service. Eaton's 1911-1912 Fall and Winter catalogue announced: "Plain Labels on Shipment. If you do not wish our name to appear on the outside of any packages, if you will request this on your order your instructions will be carried out."

Despite the hesitations of a certain portion of the population at the time, mail-order catalogues certainly transformed the way of life and the way business was done in Canada. In a sense, catalogue shopping marked the beginning of true mass consumerism.

The choice of articles that can be purchased today over the Internet and sent through the mail is unimaginable: computers, the urine of a mare in heat, baseballs, maple syrup, CBC or Cirque du Soleil products . . . CPM (CD)

HOME DELIVERY

Bianca Gendreau

We often say "mailman" or "postman," but, of course, the proper term to use is "letter carrier," the term that Canada Post endorses and that is, after all, more appropriate, given the number of women who do this job today. But until the 1960s, the general belief seemed to be that women couldn't manage the heavy mailbags or icy sidewalks. Aside from a few brief periods, such as during the two World Wars, there were few "mailwomen" until recent times.

In any case, the letter carrier plays an important role in our everyday lives, whether or not we have met him or her. In good weather or bad, this faithful person delivers our letters, magazines and bills, our good or bad news right to our mailboxes. And since we have grown up with this daily ritual, we imagine that it has been going on forever.

Actually, it was only on October 1, 1874, that free home delivery was first introduced to certain big towns. The first city to enjoy such a service was Montreal; Toronto followed six months later. A dozen years later, however, there were still many city people who rented post office lock boxes. In 1886, the postmaster of Toronto, Thomas C. Patteson, issued a letter extolling the virtues of the new system, "free delivery" that is "accurate and efficient." He added that "complaints and inquiries in regard to the delivery of these letters do not exceed the 1/4 of 1 per thousand." The letter expresses his hope that those who have hired lock boxes "may be induced to give free delivery by Carrier a trial." His acknowledgement that "many persons still cling to the old custom of using a box in the Post Office" suggests that collecting mail at the post office was a habit well anchored in the lives of his customers.

Facing page: Various models of personal letter boxes. CPM (CD)

Below: Employees of Station F, Montreal, with their postmaster. Joseph Damase Arthur Antonio Lavigne, second from the right in the front row, started working for the post office on April 26, 1910, and continued for forty years and eleven months. CPM 1992.181.5

Above: A father-and-son tradition. Left, James Robert Banguay; right, William Edward Banguay, who retired from the post office after thirty-eight years of service; and centre, their father, Samuel Banguay, posing proudly in his handsome letter carrier's uniform. CPM (CD)

Above: Joseph Damase Arthur Antonio Lavigne took such pride in his work that he posed proudly in front of a mirror in his uniform and had this photograph printed as a postcard. CPM 1992.181.2

Top left: Letter box from the late nineteenth century. These small boxes were mounted on lampposts or telegraph poles in urban areas where mail volume was low.
CPM 1974.862.1 (CD)

We can get some idea about what the first letter carriers were like by reading anecdotes in the newspapers of the times. In Dartmouth, Nova Scotia, in 1902, a letter carrier tells of his difficulties in delivering mail through snow-covered streets after a snowstorm. He also talks about being loaded down with catalogues, advertising flyers and newspapers, especially during the Christmas season, and says that most of the men carrying mail have been "distance runners or athletes in general." Relay boxes did not exist yet, and each letter carrier had to carry his mailbag the whole length of his route.

A municipality had to meet certain criteria if it wanted to have mail delivery. In 1924, it was stipulated that the population of the city must number between ten and twelve thousand persons; the urban community must be compact in surface area; the names of the streets must be posted at intersections; the houses must have street addresses; there must be sidewalks; and residential letter boxes must be installed in front of each house.

If there was no residential mailbox, the letter carrier had to ring the doorbell and await the response, but apparently homeowners had to be cajoled a bit before they agreed to install mailboxes. On June 1, 1898, the postmaster of

Brantford, Ontario, posted a notice asking local residents to please "hav[e] a place for the reception of their mail matter," which would "enable everyone to secure their mail earlier, save themselves the great annoyance of having to attend the doorbell at every ring, insure the safe delivery of letters when temporarily absent, and assist in making rapid delivery a permanent success."

The Letter Carrier's Duties

When he was hired, the letter carrier received *Instructions to Letter Carriers*, issued by the Post Office Department. In the 1912 booklet, certain directives were directly related to the performance of his tasks, such as not to hold another job that could infringe on his duties, not to be absent without leave, to be punctual. Others were of a more personal nature: it was against regulations to consume alcoholic beverages, whistle or smoke while working; employees were asked to be respectful towards their fellow citizens and their superiors, to wait a reasonable length of time after ringing the doorbell, and to avoid unnecessary conversation while sorting mail in the post office. The importance of maintaining confidentiality was mentioned several times.

Although door-to-door delivery was the most visible part of a letter carrier's work — a walk of seven to ten kilometres a day with fifteen-kilogram bags — other tasks were also required. Early in the morning, before leaving the post

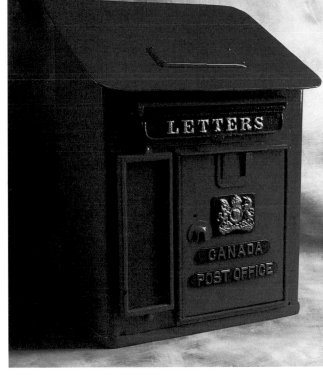

This mailbox, used in the 1930s, had to be installed on a red post.
CPM 1977.13.1 (CD)

Souvenir photo of the letter carriers at the Ottawa post office, 1914. CPM 1977.106.1

Letter carriers in front of the Besserer Street post office in Ottawa, around 1950. CPM 99-P0005

office, the letter carrier did the final sort, organizing letters, newspapers, small parcels and periodicals according to his route.

And everything had to be done rapidly: reading the address carefully, putting aside letters that were undeliverable because of errors or earlier improper sorting, completing incomplete addresses, going to the counter to pick up registered mail and insured parcels, and at the same time memorizing the changes of address of people along the route.

This was how it was done in 1920, and this is how it is still done today. In the morning, the post office sometimes looks like a battlefield. Letter carriers have their individual habits and prepare their satchels according to their own methods, but all of them know that the mail has to get out.

A Familiar Uniform

The first uniforms, dating back to the 1880s, were rather military in appearance: navy blue from head to toe, a brass nameplate with the initials CPO (Canada Post Office) and a personal identification number on the collar, and another monogram attached to the front of the kepi, the military-style cap.

After 1900, when free delivery was spreading through major cities across Canada, the number of letter carriers increased dramatically. The Post Office Department decided to provide them with the numerous necessary articles of clothing. The letter carrier's wardrobe would now boast a serge tunic and pants, a wool jacket and pants, a summer jacket, an overcoat, a raincoat, a summer hat, a kepi and a fur hat, a belt, leather gaiters, boots, copper

Mailbag from 1919, used to transport mail from one post office to another. CPM 1974.496.1 (CD)

Above: The mail processing plant in Vancouver is highly mechanized, but there are still plenty of people around to make sure the work of the machines is going smoothly. (LG)

Top right: An operator at the Halifax mail processing plant. The letter sorting machine sorts each letter into one of the approximately two hundred and fifty destination boxes that correspond to the neighbourhoods or streets of recipients. The lot from each box is bundled and sent to the proper postal station, where the letter carrier will do the final sort. (JS)

Right: One of the gems of the Canadian Postal Museum collection, this mailbox for letters and parcels is from the 1910-1920 period. Some had wooden bases under the legs to make them more stable, but the harsh climate obliged designers to replace these with metal plates. CPM 1985.117.1 (CD)

LETTERS

CANADA
POST·OFFICE

NEXT
COLLECTION

HOME DELIVERY

monograms, and a clothes brush. The rule was strict: no sloppiness allowed. The uniform was mandatory; jackets had to be buttoned up and shoes shined. The letter carrier also had to be neat and clean in appearance and have short hair and a well-trimmed beard or be clean-shaven. The reason was made clear: a letter carrier who is neat in appearance is a sign of good service; one with sloppy clothes suggests sloppy service.

The restrictions imposed by World War II and the shortage of textiles forced the Post Office Department to adopt the colour grey for uniforms. At the beginning of the fifties, however, blue returned permanently. A cap replaced the kepi, a red stripe was added to the outseam of the pants, and the jacket was dressed up with red piping.

Since about 1980, improved fabrics have altered the letter carrier's uniform considerably. Clothes that are warm and waterproof but can "breathe" and are comfortable and washable make up the twenty-first-century uniform. And although the uniform has become less military and more casual, it still plays an important symbolic role.

The Letter Carrier in the Community

Many letter carriers are conscious of the role they play in the community. They keep an eye on "their" neighbourhood, and their daily visits are reassuring for residents. Over time, they sometimes develop close ties with those they serve. People eagerly await their arrival; teenagers greet them — sometimes with snowballs — and dogs signal their feelings with wagging tails or growls. As for children, they become particularly anxious about the letter carriers' comings and goings around Christmas-time, when their letters to Santa Claus are in the mail.

Facing page, clockwise from top left: The oldest letter carrier's uniform in the collection of the Canadian Postal Museum, circa 1890. CPM 1974.502.1. *Rain cape dating from the 1930s.* CPM 1995.75.3. *At the beginning of the 1950s, the red trim was added to the uniform's pants and jacket.* CPM 1983.85.1. *When women became letter carriers in 1965, a new hat was designed to replace the familiar cap.* CPM 1974.672.1 (CD)

Often letter carriers choose their occupation in order to work outside in the fresh air; these two take their daily walks up and down the streets of Halifax. (JS)

ESTABLISHMENT OF FREE POSTAL DELIVERY IN CANADIAN CITIES

1874	Montreal
1875	Toronto, Quebec City, Ottawa, Hamilton, Saint John, Halifax
1876	London
1882	Winnipeg, Kingston
1888	Victoria
1895	Vancouver
1907	Edmonton, Calgary, Stratford, Saint-Hyacinthe, Trois-Rivières, Peterborough, Sherbrooke, Guelph, Charlottetown, Windsor
1908	St. Catharines, Sarnia, Fort William, Port Arthur, Moncton
1909	Regina
1910	Hull, Saskatoon
1911	Lethbridge, Niagara Falls
1912	Sault Ste. Marie
1913	Fredericton
1917	Shawinigan
1921	Pembroke
1922	Waterloo

A DAY IN THE LIFE

Ninon Hotte has been a letter carrier in Gatineau, Quebec, for six years. Her workday begins at the post office. When she arrives, the mail for her route has already undergone many stages of the sorting process. She puts her mail in order, packs her satchel and prepares to make her deliveries. Then she drives to her route in a Canada Post truck. Her father, Raymond Hotte, was a postmaster in Gatineau, and as a child, Ninon always admired the letter carriers' uniforms. Now she has her own and wears it with pride. (SD)

WARTIME MAIL: LOVE *and* LIFE *on the* LINE

John Willis

Canada's participation in World War I and World War II left profound traces in the memories of those who fought and those who stayed behind. The expenditure of effort, money and human lives was unprecedented, but, although the wars stretched the resources and the patience of the nation to the limits, Canada's social and political fabric emerged whole.

What enabled Canadians to survive these dramatic incursions into their otherwise peaceful lives? Possibly it was as basic as their ability to keep in touch with their loved ones and friends. Whether they were overseas in the trenches, crouched in a bomb shelter, huddled in a prison camp or laden with worry in Canada, the constant stream of letters that flowed between home front and battle front represented a remarkable achievement in communication that helped Canadians, individually as well as collectively, to keep their sense of balance.

The Morale Department

Twentieth-century war was total war, and citizens and soldiers alike had to be whipped into shape. In Canada, the government sought total commitment through a strategy of propaganda and information management as well as through control of all media. In World War I, the cinema was carefully watched; during World War II, radio broadcasts were scrutinized. In 1915, Canadian troops were deprived of their cameras to prevent them from taking pictures of the wrong things. During both wars, the government manufactured visual propaganda promoting the war effort, aided by public and private companies whose advertising campaigns extolled patriotic duty. Citizens were called upon to help win the wars by writing letters to soldiers to boost their morale. The imagery of the posters in support of letter writing was vivid and to the point.

The single most important factor in the morale-boosting program may well have been the Canadian Postal Corps, created in 1911 to make sure the all-important letters to and from the troops overseas were delivered. For the men

Facing page: Selected letters of Herman Leishman to Joan Corrigan, World War II. CPM (CD)

WRITING PAPER WAS NOT ALWAYS EASY TO GET ON THE BATTLEFIELD

Herman Dobson wrote to Muriel Macfie of his travails in October 1918: "No doubt you will say, goodness me! Where ever did I get this paper from? Well I'll tell you as near as I can. During the past month we have been doing some very fast marching after Fritz and are still doing so. Naturally we have a terrible job trying to get writing paper and such like, so we are obliged to get the best we can. So last night we marched farther on towards Germany and stopped in this fair sized town somewhere in France previous to going over the top. So today I rustled about and found what I could. And this paper is one of the things I salvaged. Now I have paper but no envelopes so I'll just write this letter and take a chance on getting envelopes. That's the very best I can do. I do wish I had some ink in my pen, then I could use it. I'm sure this writing, or scribbling I should say, will be pretty well obliterated by the time it gets to you."

Canadian Postal Corps crest. CPM 1974.2307.1 (CD)

Right: Battle dress jacket issued to Corporal Lucien Brunet of the Postal Corps on his return to Canada. Brunet spent much of the war in a Japanese prisoner-of-war camp. CPM 1984.38.5 (CD)

Below centre and right: World War II posters encouraged Canadians to write to the troops in the belief that letters from home improved morale and that good morale among the soldiers in turn would help win the war. centre: CPM 1994.66.11 (CD); right: CPM 1994.66.8 (Harry Foster)

in the field and the loved ones left behind, the Postal Corps — also known as the "morale department" — was the vital link in the communication chain. Its motto was *Servire Armatis,* or "We Serve the Forces."

During World War II, the headquarters of the Canadian Postal Corps was the five-storey Base Post Office on Nicholas Street in Ottawa. To facilitate processing and security, all mail for Canadian military personnel serving overseas passed through this post office, and, on the top floor, censors checked incoming mail destined for German prisoners of war in Canada. Parcel processing took up two entire floors. It seems there was no end to what families were willing to send servicemen overseas: cooked eggs preserved in Crisco, chocolate, sweets, shaving cream, maple syrup, bath towels. When

foods such as lobster and codfish were sloppily packed, the parcel staff were the first to know.

In Montreal, a special tobacco depot complemented the work of the Base Post Office. From here, cigarettes were distributed to the troops at the request of the families who brought or sent their order coupons to the depot. As the price of these cigarettes was discounted for the troops, special care was required to make sure they didn't fall into the hands of civilians.

Across Canada, members of the Postal Corps were stationed on virtually every military base, and were responsible for sorting mail to and from airmen, sailors and soldiers. Overseas in England, the major mail distribution centre was in an old hair-cream factory in Wembley, near London. As many as half a million Canadian troops were massed in England just before the Normandy assault in June 1944. Small wonder that such a large factory was pressed into service for the handling of the huge stacks of mail.

In addition to being stationed in England, members of the Postal Corps accompanied the army from North Africa up the Italian peninsula in 1943 and across from Normandy to Belgium and Holland the following year. As a rule, the members of the Postal Corps worked behind the lines, but the staff was vulnerable to the hazards of war, especially from enemy warplanes.

Catherine Armstrong recalls one near miss in Antwerp:

> "I was in the mess one night. All of a sudden, a chap writing to his wife — his name was Coopman — jumped up and threw me on the ground. At the same instant, the whole side of our building was bombed. One of the second buzz bombs landed on the British and American Postal units just across the street. They were demolished."

Below: Various military post office cancellation hammers. CPM (CD)

Apart from death and disability, the ultimate hazard for a Postal Corps member was to be taken prisoner. Lucien Brunet was just twenty-three years old when he enlisted in the Postal Corps. In November 1941, he left Vancouver with the ill-fated C-Force, a contingent of nineteen hundred Canadian

Facing page, far left: The thousands of letters sent overseas caused logistical problems, so in November 1941, a lightweight system was introduced. Letters headed for the same general area were opened and microfilmed; each reel could hold as many as fifteen hundred messages. Upon arrival, the messages were printed and distributed to the soldiers. NAC/C-146532

Above: Kenneth Edgar Clayton-Kennedy writing a letter in the field, World War I. Royal Canadian Air Force, Squadron 15, 19900346-032, © Canadian War Museum

Top right: Writing a letter from the battlefront in the First World War. 19920044-504, © Canadian War Museum

troops sent to reinforce Hong Kong. On Christmas Day, Hong Kong fell to the Japanese, and Brunet, along with sixteen hundred other Canadians, was taken prisoner for the duration of the war.

Conditions in the prisoner-of-war camps in Hong Kong were harsh; disease was rampant, the diet meagre. Parcels destined for the prisoners of war and shipped via the Red Cross rarely reached them. Letters were few and far between. Ford Martyn received the mail his parents had sent him only after the war had ended. His parents never heard a thing from him during the entire time he was imprisoned.

"All my thoughts upon him run . . ."

Soldiers wrote home to reassure the folks and because they were told they should. Writing soothed their nerves as well as keeping them in touch with loved ones, the ones they were fighting for. Ultimately, their morale hung from the tips of their pens, which they applied to blank pages whenever they could be found to set down their messages of love and hope, pain and despair.

In 1916, Captain Douglas Darling, a Scottish-born Canadian serving in the Canadian Machine Gun Corps, began

Left: Plaque commemorating postal clerks who served as soldiers and died in the Great War, 1914-1918. CPM 1974.2180.1 (CD)

Facing page: Bringing up mail from a dugout, September 1918. NAC/PA-003211

a correspondence with Bee Twiss, his English bride-to-be, which lasted two years. At the outset of their correspondence, he addressed her as "My dearest sister," but soon the correspondence heated up. By February 1917, she had become "my darling" and he was "your own loving Douglas." He now quoted French verse to his long-distance sweetheart:

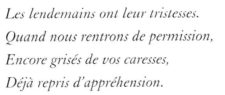

Les lendemains ont leur tristesses.
Quand nous rentrons de permission,
Encore grisés de vos caresses,
Déjà repris d'appréhension.

(Every tomorrow has its sadnesses. When we return from leave, still feeling the flame of your embraces, already fear returns.)

Herman Leishman, of Dean Lake, Ontario, joined the army early in 1942 and shortly after began writing to Joan Corrigan in Mindemoya, on Georgian Bay. His first letter to her from Camp Borden was fifteen pages long, and he wrote other, shorter letters as he made his way to Halifax and thence overseas. This being the first time he had travelled away from his home, his letters expressed his sense of wonder as he

Facing page: Canadian Postal Corps personnel. CPM except top left NAC/PA-061630

Paul Triquet sent postcards to his family as though he was on a tour of Europe, but his words belied his true situation. CPM (CD)

A World War I "postie" arrives with letters and parcels at the Canadian Military Hospital in Troyes, France.
Isaacson Collection, Canadian Nurses Association

discovered the charm of the Quebec winter ("The people all travel by horse-sleighs") and, later on, the scenery of England. Although he was not supposed to reveal the name of the ship carrying him across the Atlantic, he managed to evade the censor by inserting a crest bearing the name of the ship, *Stewardess*, into one of his letters. "Hi, my soldierette" and "Love, your apple dumpkin" testify to the warmth of their relationship, which still glows seven decades after his death in Sicily in 1943.

The mail carried sad news as well as words of love. "War is hell. You can't believe how low a man comes in a battle, the same as a beast." In 1917, Frank Maheux graphically depicted his situation to his wife back home in Canada: "The Germans . . . came in bunches like mosquitoes, but only a few came in my trenches, and they were dead way before they touched the bottom." In 1943 in a different war, the horror was the same. Herman Leishman wrote to Joan Corrigan: "I spent about half a day last week that I hope I never have to live over again, the Heines really gave us dirt, but that's war."

The horror of war numbed the mind and thickened the skin. Claude Williams, a former medical student, wrote this ironic missive to his mother in November, 1916:

> You can hardly move anywhere without stepping into a pile of bones or some other sign of your dearly beloved departed. . . . You know how seemingly morbid I am about stiffs, etc., well, I used to go searching about everywhere for good specimens for my bone collection. I now have nearly a whole skeleton rigged up under my bed; the worst of it is, he is a composite of French and Hun. I don't know whether that will agree or not, I will have to put a little English in to temper it down.

Horrors and absurdities undermined morale on both sides of the battlefield. Austro-Hungarian military postal censors began picking up strong indications of anti-war sentiment during the latter phases of World War I. In Canada, war-weariness eventually manifested itself. One mother wrote to her son in 1917 to tell him her plans to arrange compassionate leave for him:

Je t'envoie aux quatre
rouleau de film
les quelles tu
voudras bien faire
développer desuite
Ce sont de poses
prise à Paris sur
très l'autre
a eu été
sont sommes.
Maintenant
sur le bord
Au loet —Émile

Left: Postal Corps members celebrate
V-E Day in Belgium, May 5, 1945.
"We were just sitting there, relaxing,
enjoying ourselves. The people from
the little village started gathering
around, and they're yattering away in
French and Flemish. We didn't know
what they were talking about at
first, until finally I said, 'Listen to
what they're saying, La guerre est
finie! The bloody war's over!'"
CPM

Above: Émilien Brousseau (second row, sixth from left) poses
elatedly with members of his ambulance unit in Paris in May
1945. He wrote to his girlfriend back home in Amos, Quebec,
"I am sending you four rolls of film, which you will be most
kind to develop straight away. Three were taken in Paris, and
the other in Aix." Private collection

[Paddy] says he can get you leave under similar circumstances.
. . . You can get away for the worst of the winter and perhaps
be home for Xmas. . . . He wants to start proceedings to
accomplish this at once on his return. He says he will first write
your commanding officer stating you are urgently needed at
home owing to your parents' ill health or some such reason.

"The Bloody War's Over…"

The wars eventually ended in 1918 and 1945, and there was dancing in the
streets across Canada and overseas. There was an enormous sense of joy and
relief and a willingness to start over. Renewal would focus on life itself.

Above: Postcard of young Bobby
Willis and his mother Elaine on
Christmas Eve, sent January 5,
1948, from Wengen, Switzerland.
The war was two and a half years
gone; without fearing for their
safety, Canadians could make the
grand tour of Europe and send their
best wishes home by post. Most of
the soldiers were out of uniform and
returned home, young couples could
think of starting families, and the
baby boom was underway. Private
collection

ART AND THE POST

Chantal Amyot

Artists search enthusiastically for a suitable medium for their creations: they draw or paint on temple walls, on every sort of fabric, in religious books, on human skin, on advertising signs, on cupboard doors. The year 1840 saw artists staking out new territory for their creations — a small space, granted, but one with global implications: the postage stamp. Different artists were gradually adopting materials and instruments of the postal service in order to invest them with their own creative talent.

The primary role of the postage stamp is practical. However, from the start, stamps have also represented the country of issue, and countries have vied for excellence in using artistic imagination to make these modest pieces of paper into fitting ambassadors for their culture.

In our day, artists involved in making postage stamps can call upon a large selection of techniques and media. A touch of a computer key is all that is needed to reduce just about any pictorial work to the size of a postage stamp and to visualize the final product instantly. A hundred and fifty years ago, though, the process of etching and engraving was much longer and more laborious. In the twentieth century, these techniques were joined by lithography, photoengraving, computer generated design and even the making of holograms. The media used to create postage stamps have become numerous: behind these little adhesive squares is hidden intense creativity and precision work.

As well as reproducing masterpieces of Canadian art, postage stamps have, themselves, been renowned pieces of art. The January 8, 1929, issue depicting the *Bluenose* of Nova Scotia is one of the best known and most appreciated Canadian stamps. The artist, engraver Harold

Below: Canada as seen by its artists: each of these twelve postage stamps from a 1982 commemorative issue illustrates a scene from one of the ten provinces or two territories: Yukon (A.Y. Jackson), Quebec (Adrien Hébert), Newfoundland (Christopher Pratt), North West Territories (René Richard), Prince Edward Island (Molly Lamb), Nova Scotia (Alex Colville), Saskatchewan (Dorothy Knowles), Ontario (David Milne), New Brunswick (Bruno Bobak), Alberta (Illingworth Kerr), British Columbia (Joe Plaskett), Manitoba (Lionel LeMoine FitzGerald). CPM (CD)

Facing page: FUTUREPOST, *acrylic on wood and scrap metal, 1992, by Canadian artist Joe Fleming.* CPM 1993.82.1 (CD)

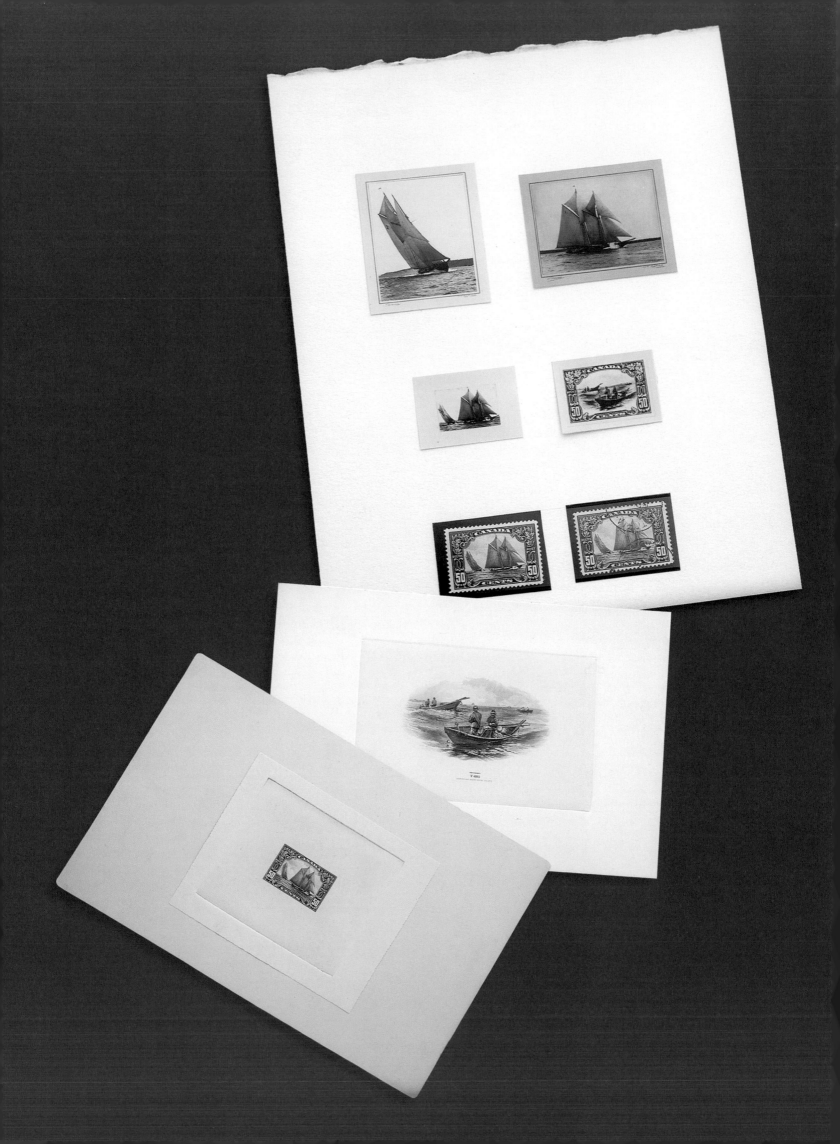

Osborn (not Charles Savage, as we long believed) had first proposed an illustration of fishing boats, as the maquette shows, but for some unknown reason this image was not retained. Because of this maquette, we can follow the evolution of the artist's work: the border created for the first proposal was kept, while the central image was replaced by a montage of two photographs by a commercial photographer from Halifax, W. R. MacAskill. Each photo shows the same boat from a different angle, and these two views of the *Bluenose* appear on the stamp.

Whether they were designed to commemorate the opening of cultural institutions across the country, to illustrate a particular event, or to present our artists to the world, many stamp issues have celebrated the creative genius of Canadian artists. From Cornelius Krieghoff to Bill Reid to Alfred Pellan, the richness and variety of Canadian artistic production are obvious when we look at the work featured on postage stamps.

Canada Post sometimes commissions works from artists. In 1984, they commissioned a series of twelve scenes from Quebec artist Jean Paul Lemieux for a special issue celebrating Confederation. Unlike paintings that can be viewed in museums and galleries, this collection is unique because the artist has worked on an imposed subject rather than from a creative impulse. Furthermore, throughout his work, the artist has kept in mind the fact that his work will be printed in miniature, reproduced in several million copies and seen by millions of people. Jean Paul Lemieux's scenes, each representing a province or territory, reveal his vision of our country.

Above, from left to right, the Canadian artworks represented on these stamps are: The Wood Bison, *Robert Bateman;* The Sprinter, *Robert Tait McKenzie;* Big Raven, *Emily Carr;* The Farmer's Family, *Bruno Bobak;* A Meeting of the School Trustees, *Robert Harris;* Le pavot bleu (Blue Poppy), *Claude A. Simard;* April in Algonquin Park *and* Autumn Birches, *Tom Thomson.* CPM (CD)

Facing page: Elements representing the process involved in creating the Bluenose *stamp, issued on January 8, 1929.* CPM 1999.109.1-3 (CD)

Set of first day covers from the Masterpieces of Canadian Art series. The Owl, *by Kenojuak Ashevak, appears on the first cover. Among the other artists are Alfred Pellan, David Milne, Frederick Varley, Bill Reid and Walter J. Phillips.* CPM (CD)

The three Christmas 1982 stamps feature Nativity figurines created by artist Hella Braun, of Kitchener, Ontario, photographed by Bert Bell.
CPM 2000.3.1-29 (CD)

Right and top: The 1976 series of Christmas stamps show Canadian stained glass windows representing the Nativity. The twenty-cent stamp reproduces a round stained glass work by Canadian artist Yvonne Williams. CPM 1984.20.1 (CD)

The Medium and the Message of the Mail

If the vast world of the post enabled visual art to find a new niche, the inverse is also true, since art has often borrowed images and materials from the postal domain. First of all, there are paintings of subjects related to the post — a woman reading a letter, a still life including a pile of envelopes bearing seals. A gallery without at least a few examples of the sort would be unusual indeed.

Another category of artwork, albeit less well known, uses postal products — letter paper, envelopes, stamps, seals — as a medium or surface for the work. When they first appeared on the market, postage stamps immediately captured the imagination of artists, and some used them as a decorative element in their work. Postage stamps have also been used to paper walls or to decorate furniture or other domestic articles.

Mixed-media works — which connect materials and media in varied and unexpected ways — have been integrated into contemporary artistic conventions. The Canadian Postal Museum collection includes contemporary art works that incorporate postal elements. The most common way of doing this is to use postage stamps in the iconography of the work, stamps chosen for their rich colour, for their shape or for the subject represented on them.

Photograph of a complete set of bedroom furniture decorated with two million postage stamps, published in the British magazine Strand *in 1898.* McGill University Libraries

Smiles, *a 1991 work by Manitoban Edna Myers, is part of a series of works representing the artist's living room. Each piece is composed of a postage stamp, a poem, an engraving and a pastel drawing.* CPM 1992.184.10 (CD)

Above: In 1998, Canada Post issued a series of postage stamps to honour the Automatistes, a group of artists from Montreal, in commemoration of the fiftieth anniversary of their Refus Global *manifesto. Among the works in this series are a painting by Paul-Émile Borduas, instigator of the manifesto, as well as works by Jean-Paul Riopelle, Fernand Leduc, Jean-Paul Mousseau, Pierre Gauvreau, Marcelle Ferron and Marcel Barbeau.* CPM (CD)

Facing page, bottom left: Ed Varney, Variations on the Mona Lisa. *Participating artists (as represented from the left column): Cracker Jack Kid, Henri Robideau, Ruud Janssen, Jesús Galdámez, Fredo Ojda, Alexandre Iskra; Aaron Flores, Daniel Daligand, Phyllis Cairns, Brian Pitt, Steen Krarúp, Bálint Szombathy; Stephen Denslow, Helmut Zielke, Karsten Matthes, Anna Banana, Mark Dicey, Vittore Baroni; Ko De Jonge, Gail Pocock, Private World, Lunar Suede, Henning Mittendorf, Ladislav Guderna; Paolo Cantarutti, Hermann Bödecker, Musicmaster, John Evans, Gaetano Colonna, Melissa Wraxall; Fran and Paul Rutovsky, Buz Blurr, Diana Durrand, Peter Dickson, Carolyn Rowney, Ed Varney.* Produced by Ed Varney. Published by the Museo Internacionale de Neu Art and the Surrey Art Gallery. CPM 1995.10.137 (CD)

Facing page, bottom right: Zer's more horses asses in zee world zan zer iz horses. *Artistamp sheet by Anna Banana.* International Art Post Vol. 6 No. 2, December .93. Sheet 6/6 by A. Banana, ISSN 0-845-6312. © 1993 Banana Productions, P.O. Box 3655, Vancouver, B.C., Canada V6B 3Y8. CPM 1995.10.104 (CD)

From top to bottom and left to right, the Canadian works appearing on these stamps are: The Ice Cone, Montmorency Falls, *Robert C. Todd;* Un village des Laurentides (Village in the Laurentian Mountains), *Clarence A. Gagnon;* Isles of Spruce, *Arthur Lismer;* Nativité (Nativity), *Jean Paul Lemieux;* Sans titre (Untitled) No. 6, *Paul-Émile Borduas;* À la Baie Saint-Paul (At Baie Saint-Paul), *Marc-Aurèle Fortin;* The Blacksmith's Shop, *Cornelius Krieghoff;* Self Portrait, *Frederick H. Varley;* Indian Encampment on Lake Huron, *Paul Kane;* Retour des champs (Return From The Harvest Field), *Marc-Aurèle de Foy Suzor-Côté;* The Fathers of Confederation, *Robert Harris;* Bird Spirit, *Doris Hagiolok;* Shaman, *Simon Tookoome;* Return of the Sun, *Kenojuak Ashevak;* Sedna, *Ashoone Kiawak;* Five Eskimos Building an Igloo, *Abraham of Povungnituk;* Summer Tent, *Kiakshuk.* CPM (CD)

But trust artists to explore every creative avenue! In the case of Montreal artist Pierre Bruneau, the medium itself comes from the post. He creates pieces directly on mailbags, envelopes or stamp albums. Bruneau uses these instead of the traditional canvas, introducing a new theme — that of the mail — into his works.

Mail Art

Finally, an international network of artists not only circulate their works by means of the postal service but involve the post in the creative process itself. "Mail art," as it is called, has existed since the 1950s. This "happening" in space and time gives artists the opportunity to integrate an external intervention into their work in a more or less controlled situation: the work is only completed once it has passed through the postal system. In a sense, the postmarks give it the finishing touch. The complete work consists of the container — the envelope or parcel — and the content — the letter or the artwork inserted into the package.

Other artists choose to work on envelopes, illustrating them in a totally unconventional fashion, while still others create objects with postal connotations, such as false postage stamps or postmarks.

Open to anyone who wishes to join, the mail art network is constantly growing. Both well-known and beginning artists from the four corners of the globe share their passion, their ideas and their creative journeys in this way. Fundamentally democratic, this art form offers an often moving and even troubling commentary on the social, political or economic tendencies of contemporary society. Recurring themes refer to the environment, racism, sexism, violence and art itself. The participating artists do not hesitate to shock, address or question the viewer: "Guernica, please stay to [sic] the Prado Museum" or "Dada is everywhere." Because the actual working mechanism of mail art stimulates

Two works of mail art created and exhibited during the L'art voyageur / Art Travels *festival organized by the Canadian Postal Museum in 1992. The one on top is by Jany Lavoie and that below, done on an actual blade of a circular saw, is by Anthony Guaraldo.*
CPM 1992.147.1 and 1992.190.1 (CD)

dialogue, certain works evolve as they circulate: a recipient might add his comments and put the work back into circulation. This form of expression allows artists not only to give their opinion on social and political tendencies but also to open up the debate on such issues.

Work of Montreal artist Pierre Bruneau: message written in black India ink on a mailbag.
CPM 1996.132.1 (CD)

WHEN THE POST GOES POP!

Bianca Gendreau

Maybe you've seen them — *Diva, Il Postino, You've Got Mail*. Completely different in style and origin, these films have all been very popular and have at least one more thing in common: the importance that the exchange of letters and messages plays in the plot. Dozens of other films have a similar development, and so do popular songs. In fact, the theme of mail appears in numerous aspects of our daily life, including sports, music and television series. Designers use mail as inspiration for their graphics, as do marketing and advertising specialists.

Ceramic stamp box in the shape of an envelope. CPM 1994.70.1 (CD)

The acts of writing and receiving letters are no less marvellous for being so common, and they have been important for centuries. Because they carry such meaning, are such signifying acts, popular arts make ample reference to them to express a group's beliefs, styles and values. Certain familiar images related to the world of the mail — the letter carrier and the dog, the mailbox, the stamped envelope — have become veritable icons. Even computers, so far removed from the material restrictions of letter paper, use the image of an envelope to say, "You've got (electronic) mail."

An icon in contemporary culture is an image whose emotional or intellectual connotations surpass the object's physical nature or its common use. These images carry meanings determined by our mentality: sets of truths and fictional meanings, of traditions and styles, of the past and the present. Why do some objects acquire the status of icon? Because what they evoke is understood instantly by a large number of people. A quill, for instance, is used often to represent romantic verse.

Facing page: Various Christmas decorations, with Santa Claus as the Great Letter Carrier. CPM (CD)

Although greeting cards have to go through the many steps of the postal system in order to reach their destinations, they are often illustrated by postal themes. Christmas cards show rural mailboxes overflowing with cards and gifts. Here, the postal symbol is a perfect illustration of the warm affection conveyed by taking the time to write and to send a card.

The Canadian Postal Museum collection includes many objects that bear witness to the links between mail and popular culture. Engaging and often light-hearted, they reflect the degree to which postal images have become symbols in a universal language.

Letter Carrier Plus Dog Equals . . .

The letter carrier is the symbol of the messenger *par excellence*; he or she is the human link between two people who correspond because they are separated geographically. The image of the letter carrier ringing the doorbell goes beyond factual information; it instantly evokes the pleasure of receiving a letter.

But the letter carrier symbolizes another cultural type as well: the responsible, hard-working, reliable individual of good will. Letter carriers are often linked to dogs, since together the two form an indivisible pair in the collective imagination. They go together as salt and pepper shakers or as bookends, they advertise house paint or pants made of some new weather-resistant material — the list seems endless.

In children's imagery, the letter carrier is a common figure, sometimes depicted as a cuddly animal bringing good news to little friends. Many greeting cards present cute bunny rabbits and gentle teddy bears delivering messages, their task signified by the objects universally associated with letter carriers: a mailbag, a cap and a badge.

Right: A picture frame and playing cards with postal iconography. CPM (CD)

For inspiration for their designs, toy manufacturers look to everything that holds a true fascination for children, to the heroes of their stories and legends, of course, but also to their daily universe. Toys designed to capture the world of the post often emphasize the technical aspect. Some represent miniature models of trains that are traditional, if not antique, or trucks or planes that served, in the past, to carry the mail. Child development specialists call such playthings initiation toys, because they enable children to gradually gain access to and knowledge of the adult world.

Other toys, which fall into the educational category, emphasize the characteristics of the postal system and the qualities it represents. In one game, children write messages and go through an elaborate process using a miniature post office and its accessories to get them to their destinations. Other postal games involve memorization.

The world may have changed rapidly, but some things have remained basically just as they were. That the elements of the world of the mail are so often represented in daily objects is proof of the importance that this means of communication has in our lives. Artists who find their inspiration in the world of the mail express a reality that everyone can understand. They recreate, in their works, a familiar universe.

Sheets of gift wrap with postal motifs. CPM (CD)

Above left: The work of Quebec illustrator Geneviève Côté, reproduced in thousands of copies as greeting cards. CPM 1995.79.1-2 (CD)

Facing page, top: Board games in which children play at being the letter carrier. CPM (CD)

Facing page, bottom: These toys from different countries show that all over the world children – and adults, too – are fascinated by postal vehicles. CPM (CD)

MOVING THE MAIL

Bianca Gendreau

Moving the mail effectively and efficiently from one Canadian location to another has always been a major concern. For much of its early history, delivering the mail over rough roads and according to somewhat random schedules was a complicated business. In the days when horse-drawn transportation was king, stagecoaches and sleighs reigned. Later, steam engines, railways and steamships gradually sped up the process. Finally, trucks, automobiles and airplanes gained the place of honour in the eternal search for speed and safety in the delivery of the mail.

The Days of Stagecoaches and Sleighs

Artists, travellers and military men described their adventures in horse-drawn vehicles as they travelled around a harsh, remote and sometimes even dangerous landscape in terms that give a romantic colouring to the era.

The idea of a horse-drawn carriage evokes the image of stagecoaches in western movies, pulled by four or six horses. A modest version of public transport, coaches often consisted of a large box without doors or windows, with benches inside, storage for trunks on the roof and a bench outside for the coachmen. Up to nine passengers — but sometimes fewer — and all manner of merchandise and luggage, including the precious mailbags, could fit into them, and they could slide on runners during the winter and roll on four wheels the rest of the year.

Postmasters were instructed to coat their leather mailbags in oil regularly to preserve the leather. After the 1860s, these bags were gradually replaced by canvas ones.
CPM 1974.506.1 (CD)

This postal contract, dated January 14, 1845, stipulated that "Her Majesty's Mails" were to be transported seven days a week between Kingston and Cobourg, Ontario, during the winter season, when steamship service was interrupted. William Weller would be paid five hundred pounds at the end of the contract, which also specified the schedule: each one-way trip was to be completed within twelve hours.
CPM 1974.1965.22 (CD)

Facing page: Canada Post's National Control Centre, Ottawa. (SD)

CONTRACT
FOR TRANSPORTING HER MAJESTY'S MAILS.

Before Confederation, the L.D. Geldert Western Stagecoach Company used the Concord Coach, renowned for its superior comfort, to carry passengers and mail between Halifax and Yarmouth, Nova Scotia. This model is based on a stagecoach in the Nova Scotia Museum, Halifax. CPM 1999.99.4 (CD)

Coach owners were generally true entrepreneurs, and some were jacks-of-all-trades; many were innkeepers or storekeepers as well as coach-drivers. Very quickly, running a stage line became big business, and companies sprang up to meet the demand. They followed routes between well-defined points wherever they were needed, with regular stops and according to a fixed schedule. But for this system to work, good, strong, well-fed horses were needed, and therefore post houses were established at regular intervals, often in hotels or inns. The innkeepers were responsible for caring for the horses and ensuring that enough horses were available to make up a team for the next coach coming through.

A businessman who wanted to secure a contract to carry mail between two or several post offices had to submit an application. The contract stipulated the period of time it would be in force, the schedules, the number of stops and even the type of vehicle to be used. Because of their importance, stage lines could make businessmen famous. The Royal Mail Line, well known in Ontario, was owned by William Weller, a rather colourful personality. Involved in several different commercial enterprises, he established a network of coach lines between 1829 and 1837, taking passengers and mail between Toronto, Montreal, Hamilton, Niagara Falls and Peterborough. Despite repeated warnings, he continued to be guilty of overloading his vehicles and not respecting his schedules, and the Post Office Department eventually had to withdraw his contract. Another noteworthy figure was Leonard D. Geldert. His Western Stagecoach Co. Ltd. carried passengers and mail in Nova Scotia for over twenty years.

A model of the type of mailbox which might be found near a train station around 1910. Railway mail clerks collected the mail from the box and sorted it aboard the train. A clock next to the box would indicate the time of the next pick-up. CPM 1985.160.1 (CD)

Travel Risks

To say that roads were in poor condition at the time would be an understatement. To make matters worse, stagecoaches were simple vehicles; all the bumps, potholes and other obstacles encountered along the way meant serious discomfort for the passengers, not to mention the real possibility of breakdowns and accidents. The coach could get stuck; the horses or passengers could be injured: these were things that happened, simply the risks of travelling this way. Only when the road was covered in well-packed snow did the route become a little less bumpy and the ride a little more comfortable.

In a letter dating back to 1842, a traveller relates to his correspondent some of the incidents of his recent trip. The stagecoach rolled over, and the two ladies who were travelling in the company of six gentlemen had to be extracted from a most embarrassing position: "If you was to see the ladies trying to get out from under the Gentlemen I am sure you would laugh," the author says. Still in good humour, he continues, "We had no broken legs or arms thank god."

In the winter, the vehicles were not required to follow established routes; the distance could often be shortened by cutting across fields. Fortunately, sleighs had high walls, and passengers could be bundled up and cushioned in furs. Mailbags were hung on hooks on the sides so they would not fall off the sleigh during the trip.

Cover of a catalogue from P.T. Légaré, a manufacturer of various types of sleighs including the berlot.
Ronald Chabot, Lévis. Collector of vintage catalogues. (SD)

Above left: A berlot used by the Canadian Transfer Co. Ltd., under the terms of a mail delivery contract with the Post Office Department. "Royal Mail" is inscribed on one side of it and "Poste royale" on the other.
CPM 1997.1.1 (CD)

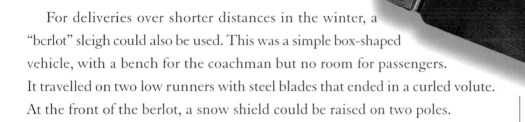

For deliveries over shorter distances in the winter, a "berlot" sleigh could also be used. This was a simple box-shaped vehicle, with a bench for the coachman but no room for passengers. It travelled on two low runners with steel blades that ended in a curled volute. At the front of the berlot, a snow shield could be raised on two poles.

Full Steam Ahead!

The railway greatly accelerated the movement of both passengers and the mail. In 1854, the Post Office Department set up railway mail cars in which mail was not only transported but also sorted between train stations. While steam locomotives crossed the country at full speed, postal employees — called railway mail clerks — crammed into the tiny train cars designed for their work. This was the way the railway postal service operated until 1971.

Railway mail clerks always have good stories to tell about their years on the railway, and pleasant memories abound. They speak of the pride and camara-

Facing page, top: RPO (Railway Post Office) cancellation hammers and handstamps. These had to be cleaned regularly in order to ensure that the postmark was legible. CPM (CD)
Bottom: Mailbag from the 1930s covered with mail clerks' messages to one another. CPM 1976.209.1 (CD)

Above: A small record book, circa 1910, logs details of a mail clerk's travels: working hours, absences, inspections, and the like. The larger accounts ledger, circa 1935, provides financial information about the railway postal service. CPM 1974.1578.1, 1974.1673.1 (CD)

Top right: Identification cards were issued to all railway mail clerks for security reasons. CPM (CD)

Top left: A souvenir photo taken by Jules-Ernest Livernois of the railway mail clerks of the Quebec division, 1923-1924. CPM 1991.36.1

derie shared by teams of clerks assigned to different routes. Their work, however, was far from easy. They had to memorize all the stops along their route and endure the cold of winter and the stifling heat of summer in the metal train cars, but their attitude helped them to deal with the challenges.

They knew how eagerly people down the line were awaiting their mail.

Ship to Shore

Rather curiously, the history of ocean mail service did not begin at sea but in the early days of the Canadian Pacific Railway. The Post Office Department considered it a natural continuation of railway service: ships took over where the railway ended. The intention was to connect the colonies to London, and thus create an "Imperial" postal route.

The first contract for mail service by ship was drawn up in 1853, but the company withdrew its offer; in 1856, the Montreal Ocean Steamship Company, known as the Allan Line, took over. The contract was for mail transport between Canada and England twice a month during the summer and once a month during the winter. The first trip was made on April 23, 1856, on the *North American*, and, at two-week intervals thereafter, on the *Canadian*, the *Anglo-Saxon* and the *Indian*. Soon they began to provide weekly service.

Ocean mail service followed the same principles as railway mail operations. The first postal employees on ships were former railway mail clerks accustomed to working in confined spaces while travelling continuously, and the administration felt that the jobs and working conditions were equivalent. However, there were real dangers associated with this new occupation. In 1864, three of the fourteen ocean mail clerks aboard ships lost their lives in shipwrecks.

Clerks had only a few days to sort over fifteen thousand letters and newspapers. The ocean mail clerk began his work in Pointe-au-Père, near Rimouski, Quebec, and did not finish until the ship reached Moville, in Ireland. He had to follow regulations and continue his work, no matter

Above right: A plate used aboard Allan Line ships, decorated with the crest of Montreal, where Allan had its headquarters (bottom). A plate made by the E.F. Bodley & Son (Longport) company in 1890 for the Canada Shipping company, Montreal, which had postal contracts (top). CPM 1974.1994.1, 1974.1995.1 (CD)

A scale model of the RMS Canadian, *of the Montreal Ocean Steamship Company (Allan Line), built for the Canadian Postal Museum in 1974 from photographs and the ship's original plans. The* Canadian *first sailed in 1856. When it sank a year later near Saint-Jean-Port-Joli, its 350 passengers were rescued and the mail was saved.* CPM 1995.83.3 (CD)

Below: A postcard and a trade card advertising the Allan Line. CPM 2000.29.1, 2000.11.1 (CD)

how rough the sea became. As he worked alone, it was impossible to hide any mistakes, and only a major incident could excuse him from completing his tasks.

The association between Allan Line and the Post Office Department lasted for over sixty years, until the company became part of the Canadian Pacific Steamship Company.

The Sky's the Limit

Although airplanes were, at first, considered a mere curiosity, it quickly became clear that this was the invention of the century. Moreover, the importance of aviation in World War I is well known. The first airlines were created, new routes were developed, and the world seemed to shrink. Pilots who had flown in combat converted to mail delivery flights, long-distance treks and air shows.

During the war, while cannons were still smoking in Europe, people had already started thinking of something new for airplanes to do in peacetime: they had the crazy, seemingly impossible dream of building an air-mail route connecting Toulouse, in the south of France, to Tierra del Fuego, at the tip of South America. Entrepreneurs by the name of Pierre-Georges Latécoère and Marcel Bouilloux-Lafont and intrepid pilots like Jean Mermoz, Antoine de Saint-Exupéry and Henri Guillaumet traced out the line between the continents. All adopted the same credo: deliver the mail, no matter what.

At the same time, economic development and the settlements spreading into new regions encouraged the Post Office Department to consider establishing airmail service in Canada. There were a few postal flights starting in 1918, but the real adventure began in 1928, when airmail routes were created between Pointe-au-Père and Montreal and then between Montreal and Toronto to speed up the receipt and delivery of transatlantic mail.

At the same time, certain airline companies transported mail to and from communities and businesses in areas inaccessible by land or water. These services were strictly controlled by the Post Office and the companies were authorized to issue "semi-official" stamps bearing their business name to pay for the service.

When the airmail delivery route was completed in 1939, it stretched from Montreal to Vancouver, and a year later, in 1940, it extended right across Canada, from Halifax to Vancouver. Over a period of ten years, new airports furnished with adequate lighting systems had been built along the way, making overnight postal flights possible.

Postmarks commemorating the first official mail flights. CPM (CD)

Facing page: Airmail bags. CPM (CD)

Whitehorse Star

WHITEHORSE, YUKON, APRIL 18, 1928

NUMBER FORTY-SIX

Yukon first flight to Atlin, B. C., Canada

...ss and Atlin Have First Visit From Airship!
...e the Yukon First Plane to Visit Important Northern Towns

...then only to be forced the town passes, particularly Whitehorse Star, carried by
...second time after during the summer season, air to Carcross and Atlin o...
...about fifteen thousands of tourists, big the first flight to these tow...
game hunters, prospectors of the first plane operatin...
and miners. this great northern secti...
the days of the fam- the Queen of the Yukon...
Atlin, British This copy made the...
impor- air and bears the...
the offices throug...

*Airline stickers
used and collected by
passengers around the world.*
CPM (CD)

*Above right: This April 13, 1928
edition of the* Whitehorse Star *was
delivered by Yukon Airways &
Exploration Co. Ltd., using its own
"semi-official" stamp.* CPM 1996.28.1.

Used with permission of the *Whitehorse Star.* (CD)

*Airmail stickers and a first flight
cover dated December 6, 1930.*
CPM (CD)

Up for Adventure

Airplanes made easy, year-round access possible to new territories previously accessible only by canoe in the summer and dogsled in the winter. Until then, the small communities in these regions were cut off from the world for several months in the winter, when mail service consisted of a few irregular dogsled visits. In 1932, Father Saindon, of Moosonee, James Bay, wrote to tell the Post-master General how isolated his missionaries felt. The mail brings them great comfort, he said, especially at Christmas and New Year's. But in 1932, they would be cut off from this consolation, a thought that tortured him, since many would not get a letter before the first week of July.

In 1930, piloting was still a great adventure. This was even truer in the great Canadian North. Pilots had to be brave, of course, but they also had to be able to solve the numerous problems that could arise and make repairs to their roughly constructed airplanes, which consisted, at the time, of a cloth-covered cabin, wooden wings, and almost no instrumentation. In these extreme weather conditions, their navigation skills had to be well honed, enabling them to trace out the rivers that would orient them in the landscape and serve as landing strips in the summer.

Men like Roméo Vachon, Art Schade, Wilfrid Reid "Wop" May, Clennell Haggerston "Punch" Dickins and others were risk-takers and adventure-lovers who enjoyed these challenges. Such "flying postmen" earned their reputation for getting the mail anywhere, one way or another.

Pilot Roméo Vachon, shown bare-headed behind the mailbags, before the inaugural flight of the Rimouski-Montreal airmail route, on May 5, 1928. There were ninety-seven such flights on Canadian Transcontinental planes that year. NAC/C-081888

Above left: A world premiere: on July 9, 1918, a woman was at the controls of a plane carrying mail. Shown here in a Curtiss Stinson Special, Katherine Stinson, an American, is about to fly the Calgary-Edmonton route. The mail is postmarked "Aeroplane Mail Service, July 9, 1918, Calgary Alberta." A crowd gathered to encourage the aviatrix during her flight, the first to transport mail in western Canada. Canada Aviation Museum, Ottawa

Above right: Canadian Transfer Co. delivery wagon, Montreal, Quebec, circa 1930. Notman Photographic Archives, McCord Museum of Canadian History, Montreal, MP-1984.105.14

But trains and planes could not entirely meet the growing needs of Canadians. With a greater volume of mail circulating, the Post Office re-examined its distribution system and decided to diversify its means of transporting the mail. When automobiles and roads improved, a solution presented itself: cars and trucks were not restricted by train routes or passenger schedules and could better fulfill the demands of the twentieth century.

At the dawn of the twenty-first century, transporting the mail presents new challenges. New issues have arisen. Always looking for ways to improve its services, the postal service is now concerned with environmental issues. Surface delivery is still the predominant means of transporting the mail, but it has a considerable impact on our environment: trucking causes pollution and damages highways. There are good reasons to reconsider railway transportation: first, technological advances have made the train system faster and more dependable, and second, wheels can be installed under containers so that they can move directly onto railways. Air transport is being enhanced by another change: the postal service is trying to reduce its dependence on passenger flights by using charter planes.

These new possibilities accompany new techniques of mail handling and tracking. Mailbags are being replaced by plastic containers, which are stackable, more durable, and can keep envelopes from being bent or folded. New mail tracking systems will soon be in use all over the country. Before

Left: A scale model of a quadricycle used to deliver mail in Toronto between 1900 and 1902. This simple vehicle, powered by a 402 cm³ one-cylinder water-cooled motor, has pedals to help the driver get up steep hills. The Post Office Department bought four of these, but the motor's lack of power and the absence of a roof and windshield to protect the driver from bad weather won out over the financial advantages. The model was built for the Canadian Postal Museum in 1974 from archival photographs. CPM 1995.83.1 (CD)

Below: Models of vehicles used by the Post Office Department in 1901. NAC/POS-003345

Right: A scale model of the first motorcar used for mail delivery. The "Locomobile" was an American design but built in Canada by the National Cycle & Automobile Co. Ltd. Steered by a handle rather than a steering wheel, it ran on two 2.5" x 3" (6.4 x 7.6 cm) steam-powered cylinders weighing only forty pounds (18 kg) in total, and it could really move: up to twenty-five miles (40 km) per hour! The basic model cost $900, not including the $100 closed box to protect the mailbags. Unfortunately, the motor got overheated, required a great deal of water every twenty miles (32 km) and tended to freeze in winter. Needless to say, its term as a postal vehicle was short-lived: it was used only between 1900 and 1902. The model was built for the Canadian Postal Museum according to archival documents and drawings. CPM 1995.83.2 (CD)

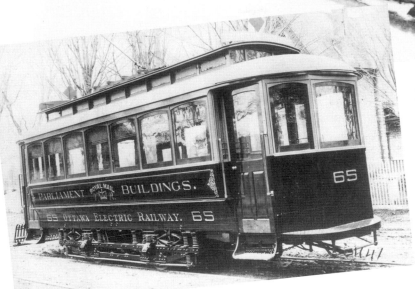

Founded in 1891, the Ottawa Electric Railway obtained a contract for exclusive services with the Post Office Department, and its first car was used for the sole purpose of transporting mailbags between the train station and the post office. In 1905, car number 65 served the Parliament Buildings. NAC/PA-143140

Top: Bombardier snowmobile, model B-12, used to carry mail between L'Anse-Saint-Jean and Port-Alfred, Quebec. J. Armand Bombardier Museum

long, senders will be able to trace their letters or parcels by means of a sophisticated system using bar codes, microprocessors and satellite transmission signals.

In order to put these progressive measures into place in the years to come, the postal service has established a system that makes Canada a world leader in the improvement of distribution and quality control. Situated in the very centre of the Canada Post corporate headquarters in Ottawa, the National Control Centre monitors tens of billions of letters and packages sent to more than twelve million addresses across the country every year. On a giant map of Canada, and with the help of advanced technology and electronic reporting systems, mail can be traced, obstacles identified and proper delivery ensured. The National Control Centre has put Canada at the leading edge of postal service technologies, and postal administrations from around the globe seek out Canada's expertise in this field.

Mail is shipped to the mail processing plant in Saint-Laurent near Montreal, in tractor-trailers. Four of the drivers are seen here, proudly posing in front of their trucks: (left to right) Glen Sutton, René Laflamme, Serge Carrière and Pierre Denis. (SD)

In the international zone of the Saint-Laurent mail processing plant, the pace is hectic between late afternoon and dawn and slower during the day. (SD)

At the Macdonald-Cartier International Airport in Ottawa, mail is unloaded from a Purolator cargo plane. The containers are specially designed to fit into this type of aircraft. Purolator has been a subsidiary of Canada Post since 1993. (SD)

Mail in Canada Post containers is loaded into the cargo hold of a passenger airplane at the Macdonald-Cartier International Airport. (SD)

MOVING THE MAIL

BIOGRAPHICAL NOTES

FRANCINE BROUSSEAU

Francine Brousseau, the Director of the Canadian Postal Museum and Director of Exhibitions, Canadian Museum of Civilization, is the editor of *Special Delivery: Canada's Postal Heritage*. An art historian with a master's degree in Public Administration, she has worked in the area of heritage and museology since 1975; associated with the Canadian Postal Museum since 1984, she has been the director since 1990. She has written several books and articles and the materials for many exhibitions, and she was responsible for the integration of the Canadian Postal Museum with the Canadian Museum of Civilization. She is a member of the board of directors of the International Association of Transport and Communication Museums and is the vice-president of the Canadian Museum Association.

CHANTAL AMYOT

With degrees in Art History and Museum Studies, Chantal Amyot has worked with the Canadian Postal Museum for twelve years, first as curator and then as Head of Public Programmes. She is now responsible for planning for the Canadian Postal Museum and Manager of Exhibitions at the Canadian Museum of Civilization. She has taken part in several major projects, including the installation of the Canadian Postal Museum in the Canadian Museum of Civilization, the production of a CD-ROM and the development of numerous exhibitions. She has also written articles on the post which have been published in specialized journals.

BIANCA GENDREAU

Bianca Gendreau holds master's degrees in History and Museum Studies. She joined the Canadian Postal Museum team in 1990 and served as assistant curator of collections and as director of public programmes before becoming the Curator of the collection in 1995. She has curated several important exhibitions at the Museum as well as travelling and virtual exhibitions. She has also published articles and given conference papers on the subject of postal history.

JOHN WILLIS

John Willis, a historian by profession and by preference, has a doctorate in Historical Geography from Université Laval. He has been with the Canadian Postal Museum, where he oversees historical research, since 1991. An enthusiast of history in general and especially social and postal history, he has written a number of articles and publications on the history of postal communications in Canada. He has worked on several major exhibitions, including the permanent exhibition, *Signed, Sealed, Delivered*, installed in 2000. He has published works in various readers and scholarly journals and contributes regularly to the postal history column of the magazine *Cap-aux-Diamants*.

CLAIRE DUFOUR

Claire Dufour took most of the photographs of the Canadian Postal Museum artifacts shown in *Special Delivery: Canada's Postal Heritage*. She has taken part in many publishing and museum projects. Her photographs have been published in prestigious magazines, including *Force* and *enRoute*, and have been featured many times in photography publications. Specializing in promotional photography, she treats each photo like a painting, engaging in play with light, mood and composition.

SELECTED BIBLIOGRAPHY

THE POST: CARRIER OF THE WORD

Beniger, James R. *The Control Revolution: Technological Change and Economic Origins of the Information Society*. Cambridge MA: Harvard University Press, 1986.

Braudel, Fernand. *Civilization and Capitalism 15th-18th Century*. Vol. 1, *Structures of Everyday Life*. New York: Harper and Row, 1981.

Crowley, David and P. Heyer. *Communication in History: Technology, Culture and Society*, White Plains NY: Longman, 1995.

Dauphin, Cécile et al. *Ces bonnes lettres : Une correspondance familiale au XIXe siècle*. Paris: Albin Michel, 1995.

Farge, Arlette. *Fragile Lives: Violence, Power and Solidarity in Eighteenth Century Paris*. Cambridge MA: Harvard University Press, 1993.

Finnegan, Ruth. *Literacy and Orality: Studies in the Technology of Communication*. Oxford: Blackwell, 1988.

Innis, H.A. *Empire and Communication*. Toronto: University of Toronto Press, 1972.

Melançon, Benoit. *Sevigne @ Internet: Remarques sur le courrier électronique*. Montréal: Éditions Fides, 1996.

PUTTING PEN TO PAPER

Anonymous. *Le secrétaire des amoureux et des gens du monde*. Montréal: Librairie Beauchemin, 1917.

Brenner, Robert. *Valentine Treasury: A Century of Valentine Cards*. Atglen PA: Schiffer, 1997.

Roger Chartier, ed. *La correspondance: Les usages de la lettre au XIXe siècle*. Paris: Fayard, 1991.

Dauphin, Cécile et al. *Ces bonnes lettres : Une correspondance familiale au XIXe siècle*. Paris: Albin Michel, 1995.

Meilleur, Jean-Baptiste. *Court traité sur l'art épistolaire*. 2nd Ed. Montréal: P. Gendron, 1849.

THE COLONIAL ERA:
BRINGING THE POST TO NORTH AMERICA

Various published series of letters were consulted, including those of the Papineau family and those of Msgr. Lartigue, the first Catholic bishop of Montreal; both series appeared in *Rapport de l'Archiviste de la Province de Québec*. Eighteenth- and early nineteenth-century newspapers published in Montreal, Toronto, Kingston, Bytown (Ottawa), Saint John and Halifax contain much material on postal matters. *Canada (Province) Legislative Assembly. Appendices and Sessional Papers*, 2nd Session, 2nd Parliament (1846), Appendix F: "Report of the Commissioners appointed to enquire into the affairs of the Post Office Department in British North America, 26 March 1846" is a vital source of information; the appendices contain a wealth of material on the maritime colonies as well as Canada.

Bérubé, G. and Marie-France Silver. *La lettre au XVIIIe siècle et ses avatars*. Toronto: Éditions du GREF, 1996.

Gadoury, Lorraine. *La famille dans son intimité: Échanges épistolaires au sein de l'élite canadienne du XVIIIe siècle*. Montréal: Hurtubise, 1998.

Harrison, Jane E. *Until Next Year: Letter Writing and the Mails in the Canadas, 1640-1830*. Hull: Canadian Museum of Civilization; Waterloo: University of Waterloo Press, 1997.

Little, J.I. *The Child Letters: Public and Private Life in a Canadian Merchant-Politician's Family, 1841-1845*.

Montreal and Kingston: McGill-Queen's University Press, 1995.

McKenna, Katherine M.J. *A Life of Propriety: Anne Murray Powell and Her Family, 1755-1849*. Montreal and Kingston: McGill-Queen's University Press, 1994.

Noël, Françoise. "Note de recherche: My Dear Eliza: The Letters of Robert Hoyle, 1831-1844," *Histoire sociale / Social History* 26:51 (May 1993): 115-130.

Smith, William. *The History of the Post Office in British North America, 1639-1870*. Cambridge: Cambridge University Press, 1920.

POSTAGE STAMPS: WINDOWS ON THE WORLD

Boggs, Winthrop S. *The Postage Stamps and Postal History of Canada*. Kalamazoo MI: Chambers, 1945; rpt. Lawrence MA; Quarterman, 1974.

Howes, Clifton A. *Canadian Postage Stamps and Stationery*. Boston: New England Stamp Co., 1911; rpt. Lawrence MA: Quarterman, 1974.

Jarrett, Fred. *Stamps of British North America*. Toronto: F. Jarrett, 1939; rpt. Lawrence MA: Quarterman, 1975.

Masse, Denis. *Le castor de Fleming et ses descendants*. Montréal: Denis Masse Éditeur, 1993.

The Sandford Fleming 3 Pence Essay. Waterford MI: Charles G. Firby Auctions, 1996.

Verge, Charles J.G. "The Six Penny Prince Consort, Stamp of Canada's Pence period," *Scott Stamp Monthly* (Dec. 1997): 41.

THE POST OFFICE: AT THE HEART OF THE NATION

Archibald, Margaret. *By Federal Design: The Chief Architect's Branch of the Department of Public Works, 1881-1914*. Ottawa: Parks Canada, 1983.

Kalman, Harold. *A History of Canadian Architecture*. Vol. 2. Toronto: Oxford University Press, 1994.

Maguire, C.R. "Canada's Post Office Architecture: The Second Empire Style, ca. 1871-1881," *Stampex* (May 24-26, 1985).

Maitland, Leslie and Randy Rostecki. "Post Offices by Thomas Fuller 1881-1896." Agenda Paper, Historic Sites and Monuments Board of Canada (June 1983).

Maitland, Leslie, Jacqueline Hucker, and Shannon Ricketts. *A Guide to Canadian Architectural Styles*. Peterborough: Broadview Press, 1992.

Thomas, C.A. "Architectural Image for the Dominion: Scott, Fuller and the Stratford Post Office." *Journal Of Canadian Art History* 3:1, 3:2 (fall 1976).

Wright, Janet, *Crown Assets: The Architecture of the Department of Public Works, 1867-1967*. Toronto: University of Toronto Press, 1997.

THE RURAL POSTMASTER

This chapter is based on information obtained from a series of oral history interviews with twenty-five former postmasters and postmistresses. Also useful is the information in the D-3 series, Record Group 3 (Archives of Canada Post and the Post Office Department) held by the National Archives of Canada. In 1993 the Canadian Postal Museum acquired all of the interior furnishings of the former post office at Val Morin Station, Quebec. This collection constitutes an excellent source of rural postal history.

Osborne, B.S. and R. Pike. "The Postal Service and Canadian Social History. Part 1: Petitions, Inspectors' Reports and the Postal Archives." *Postal History Society of Canada Journal* 35 (1983): 37-42.

Osborne, B.S. and R. Pike. "The Postal Service and Canadian Social History. Part 2: The Location Decision." *Postal History Society of Canada Journal* 41 (1985): 11-14.

Osborne, B.S. and R. Pike. "Lowering the Walls of Oblivion: The Revolution in Postal Communications in Central Canada, 1851-1911." In *Canadian Papers in Rural History*, Vol. 4, edited by Donald H. Akenson, 200-225. Gananoque ON: Longdale Press, 1984.

Willis, John. "L'importance sociale du bureau de poste en milieu rural au Canada, 1880-1945." *Histoire sociale / Social History* (May 1997): 143-168.

THE CATALOGUE: A DREAM INVENTORY

Broadfoot, Barry. *The Pioneer Years, 1895-1914. Memories of Settlers Who Opened the West*. Toronto: Doubleday, 1976.

Eaton, Flora. *Memory's Wall: The Autobiography of Flora McCrea Eaton*. Toronto: Clarke Irwin, 1956.

Emmet, Boris and J.E. Jeuck. *Catalogues and Counters: A History of Sears, Roebuck and Company*. Chicago: University of Chicago Press, 1950.

Santink, J.L. *Timothy Eaton and the Rise of his Department Store*. Toronto: University of Toronto Press, 1990.

Stephenson, W. *The Store That Timothy Built*. Toronto: McClelland and Stewart, 1969.

HOME DELIVERY

This chapter is based on oral history interviews with letter carriers in the national capital region in 1999, and on files in the National Archives of Canada, particularly the archives of the Post Office Department, RG3, Finding aid 3-5, Parts 1-2.

WARTIME MAIL: LOVE AND LIFE ON THE LINE

This chapter is based on 1995-1996 interviews with former members of the Canadian Postal Corps during World War II and on collections of correspondence, especially the Crochetière and Leishman letters, Canadian Postal Museum; the Scythes collection, Canadian War Museum; and the Frank Maheux correspondence, National Archives of Canada. Quotations from the correspondence of Captain W.D. Darling, held in the Imperial War Museum, are used by permission of his daughter, Mrs. Bee Palmer.

Comeau, Paul-André. *La démocratie en veilleuse: Rapport sur la censure: Récit de l'organisation, des activités et de la démobilisation de la censure pendant la guerre de 1939-45*. Montréal: Éditions Québec Amérique, 1995.

Greenhous, Berenton. *"C" Force to Hong Kong: A Canadian Catastrophe, 1941-1945*. Toronto: Dundurn Press, 1997.

Keshen, Jeffrey. *Propaganda and Censorship in Canada's Great War*. Edmonton: University of Alberta Press, 1996.

Litoff, J.B. and D. C. Smit. *Since You Went Away: World War II Letters from American Women on the Home Front*. New York: Oxford University Press, 1991.

ART AND THE POST

Brousseau, Francine. *Jean Paul Lemieux: His Canada*. Hull: Canadian Postal Museum, 1998.

Butor, Michel et al. *Plis d'excellence: L'extraordinaire créativité de la correspondance*. Paris: Éditions Musée de la Poste, 1994.

Leymarie, Jean. *The Spirit of the Letter in Painting*. Hallmark Cards and Skira Creations, 1961.

Massé, A. and S. McLeod O'Reilly. *L'art voyageur: Festival d'art par correspondance / Art Travels: Mail Art Festival*. Hull: Canadian Museum of Civilization, 1992.

Massé, A. and S. McLeod O'Reilly. *Collecting Passions: Discovering the Fun of Finding Stamps and Other Stuff From All Over the Place*. Illus. Norman Eyolfson. Hull: Canadian Museum of Civilization; Toronto: Key Porter Kids, 1999.

Welch, Chuck. *Eternal Network: A Mail Art Anthology*. Calgary: University of Calgary Press, 1995.

WHEN THE POST GOES POP!

Coulaud, Hervé and Sophie Nagiscarde. *Les jouets de la poste*. Paris: Maeght Éditeur, Musée de la poste de Paris, 1991.

MOVING THE MAIL

This chapter is based on oral history interviews with retired railway mail clerks, Canadian Postal Museum, 1987.

Arnell, J.C, *Atlantic Mails: A History of the Mail Service Between Great Britain and Canada to 1889*. Ottawa: Canadian Postal Museum, 1980.

Berkebile, Don H. *Carriage Terminology: An Historical Dictionary*. Washington DC: Smithsonian Institution Press and Liberty Cap Books, 1978.

McLeod O'Reilly, Susan. *On Track: The Railway Mail Service in Canada*. Hull: Canadian Postal Museum, 1992.

INDEX